HOW TO SATISFY A TAURUS

As a (self-satisfied) triple Taurus (Sun, Moon and Mercury) with Gemini as Ascendant, after reading Mary's book, *How to Satisfy a Taurus*, it doesn't at all surprise me that I am a lifelong passionate gardener and writer who deeply values the sensual world.
Celia M. Gunn, author of *A Twist in Coyote's Tale* and *Simply Totem Animals*

Mary writes with both a deep understanding and great humour. She has the ability to sum up a sign's essence in a title – no mean feat! I love the way she goes through the history of Astrology, the sign and its ruling planet. This is more than the usual superficial glance at a sign. It provides true understanding!
Ana Isabel, astrologer and presenter for My Spirit Radio

T0167552

How to Satisfy a Taurus

Real Life Guidance on How
to Get Along and Be Friends
with the 2nd Sign of the Zodiac

How to
Satisfy
a Taurus

Real Life Guidance on How
to Get Along and Be Friends
with the 2nd Sign of the Zodiac

Mary English

Winchester, UK
Washington, USA

First published by Dodona Books, 2013
Dodona Books is an imprint of John Hunt Publishing Ltd., Laurel House, Station Approach,
Alresford, Hants, SO24 9JH, UK
office1@jhpbooks.net
www.johnhuntpublishing.com
www.dodona-books.com

For distributor details and how to order please visit the 'Ordering' section on our website.

Text copyright: Mary English 2013

ISBN: 978 1 78279 152 2

A CIP catalogue record for this book is available from the British Library.

Design: Stuart Davies

Printed and bound by CPI Group (UK) Ltd, Croydon, CR0 4YY

We operate a distinctive and ethical publishing philosophy in all
areas of our business, from our global network of authors to
production and worldwide distribution.

CONTENTS

Also by Mary English

6 Easy Steps in Astrology
The Birth Chart of Indigo Children
How to Survive a Pisces (O-Books)
How to Bond with an Aquarius
How to Cheer Up a Capricorn
How to Believe in a Sagittarius
How to Win the Trust of a Scorpio
How to Love a Libra
How to Soothe a Virgo
How to Lavish a Leo
How to Care for a Cancer
How to Listen to a Gemini
How to Appreciate an Aries

This book is dedicated to:
My lovely stepson Steve
and
My wonderful husband Jonathan
You are my true soul-love and our love knows no bounds

Acknowledgements

I would like to thank the following people:

My son for being the Libran that makes me always look on the other side.

Mabel, Jessica and Usha for their homeopathic help and understanding.

Laura and Mandy for their friendship.

Donna Cunningham for her help and advice.

Judy Hall for her inspiration.

Alois Treindl for being the Pisces that founded the wonderful Astro.com website.

Judy Ramsell Howard at the Bach Centre for her encouragement.

John my publisher for being the person that fought tooth and nail to get this book published and all the staff at O-Books including Stuart, Trevor, Kate, Catherine, Maria M and Maria B, Nick, Mollie, and Mary.

Special thanks to Mary and Oksana for their welcome 'read throughs.'

And last but not least my lovely clients for their valued contributions.

Introduction

There are some days when I think I'm going to die from an overdose of satisfaction.
Salvador Dali

I love that quote from Taurus Salvador Dali. He must have known I was going to write about his Sun sign one day!

When I told my friends I was writing a book about Taurus, I got some funny emails. Here's a Pisces lady called Romana and she tells me:

'Hi Mary,
I have been married to a double Taurean (Sun and Moon) for 20 years and seem to have had a series of Taurean boyfriends before that!
How to satisfy a Taurean?
Easy!
Sex/Food – plenty of it.
Creature comforts / Quality toys, e.g. hi-fi equipment / fancy phone / gadgets.
Lots of praise and touchy-feely stuff.'

There we go! That says it in a nutshell! I don't have to write the book now...do I?

This book is the penultimate book in a series of 12 that I started when I found out that my sign still didn't seem to be understood by the general public. A sort of 'Users' Manual'.

When I finished the Pisces book, my friends and family asked me when I was going to write about 'their' sign, so here I am, having gone backwards through the Zodiac, with Taurus the 2nd sign of the Zodiac.

I am married to a Taurus too but I'd never had a Taurus

boyfriend or best friend before we met. In fact I'd hardly known any Taureans until I moved to the West Country (in England) where I now live. My homeopathic supervisor is a Taurus and she became a very dear friend, and she also, because I worked alongside her, taught me a lot about this sign. So I can safely say I am writing this from personal experience, not just from my astrological knowledge.

I did have a crush on a Taurus young man when I was a teen. My mother really liked him too. He was very popular with women. He was good friends with my older sister, who cared for him a lot, but I think he was actually a friend of my brother's. I can't remember now. What I do remember was his gentle kind manner, his impeccable taste and his obvious good looks. He also had the ability to really listen to me when I talked…which in those days was a considerable amount!

He got snapped up pretty quickly and my sister was deeply upset when his new girlfriend insisted that he break off his friendship with her. She never really forgave that, as for an Aquarius friendship is like breathing and to have that arrested was terribly upsetting.

One thing is for sure. If you're dating a Taurus, you'd better snap him up quickly as they very rarely get divorced or play the field.

If you ever log on to a dating site the ratio of Gemini/Pisces men to Taurus will be about 80:20 as Gemini/Pisces are what's called a 'mutable' sign, one that needs change. Taurus is a 'fixed' sign, one that *doesn't* like change. And one that also maybe fears change, but we will be learning more about this as we go along.

Astrology has a very ancient history and a fascinating one at that. Before we learn about the sign of Taurus, we need to under- stand a little about where Astrology came from and where it is today.

Not much has changed since its origins. The symbols we use, and the way a birth chart is calculated, are still the same as they were when the Babylonians first looked at the heavens and saw a correlation between the movement of the planets and our lives on Earth.

'As above, so below' – this is still the mantra that we abide by. But Astrology isn't a replacement for religion, even though plenty of the gods we talk about have been worshipped in the past. Now Astrology is more a way of explaining our random, pointless lives on Earth and giving them *meaning*.

Christopher McIntosh, a historian, tells about the priests in ancient Babylon in his *The Astrologers and Their Creed*:

The priests of this kingdom made the discovery, which developed into what we now call astronomy and the zodiacal system of the planets, which we call astrology today. For many generations they painstakingly recorded the movements of these heavenly bodies. Eventually they discovered, by careful calculation, that in addition to the Sun and the Moon, five other visible planets moved in specific directions every day. These were the planets that we now call Mercury, Venus, Mars, Jupiter and Saturn.

The priests lived highly secluded lives in monasteries adjacent to massive pyramidal observation towers called ziqqurats. Every day they observed the movements of the planets and noted down any corresponding earthly phenomena from floods to rebellions. They came to the conclusion that the laws which governed the movements of the stars and planets also governed events on Earth.

In the beginning, the stars and planets were regarded as being actual gods. Later, as religion became more sophisticated, the two ideas were separated and the belief developed that the god 'ruled' the corresponding planet.

Gradually, a highly complex system was built up in which each planet had a particular set of properties ascribed to it. This system was developed partly through the reports of the priests and partly though the natural characteristics of the planets. Mars was seen to be red in colour and was therefore identified with the god Nergal, the fiery god of war and destruction.

Venus, identified by the Sumerians as their goddess Inanna, was the most prominent in the morning, giving birth as it were, to the day. She therefore became the planet associated with the female qualities of love, gentleness and reproduction.[1]

Eventually Astrology made its way across the oceans to Greece, Egypt, Rome in Italy, and then to the rest of Europe, changing little in meaning and delivery in that time. Early astrologers had to be able to read and write and calculate difficult mathematical placements of the planets, something that computers now do easily. You won't have to do anything difficult to make the birth charts we're going to make in this book.

I'd like to make a few distinctions about what Astrology is, and isn't. A lot of people seem to think that Astrology is just about prediction, as if all that astrologers do all day is look 'into the future'. This is not entirely true. There are all sorts of astrologers, just as there are all sorts of people. Some astrologers are interested in the history of Astrology. Some involve themselves in counselling, or business advice, or like me write Sun sign columns in the media. Some use Astrology for personality profiling. Some are interested in psychology, health, relationships or politics, but all, mostly, are interested in the 'whys' of life and the reasons. They are interested in the *meaning* of life.

Basic Principles

When we talk about Sun signs, what we mean is the sign that the Sun (that big ball of flames) was in on the day the person was born. And Astrology isn't just about the Sun. Along with the Moon and the Sun there are at least 9 other celestial bodies in the sky that we observe and plot their paths as they orbit around the Sun: Mercury, Venus, Mars, Jupiter, Saturn and the three more recent discoveries of Uranus, Neptune and Pluto which I discussed in my books *How to Bond with an Aquarius*, *How to Survive a Pisces* and *How to Win the Trust of a Scorpio* respectively.

The planets are the bits in the sky that move, because they are orbiting, like us, around the Sun and we call them the Solar (Sun) System.

The stars, which are the twinkly bits we see at night, don't move and are like a background or backdrop to the night sky. Originally the planets moved with certain stars behind them, like a curtain, but now because of a thing called the 'precession of the equinoxes', the stars and the planets are no longer aligned in the same way.

So an astronomer might say you're a Pisces, when we might say you're a different sign as everything has shifted. There are even astrologers that still use the stars as a backdrop. They are called Sidereal Astrologers and have different dates to our western astrological date.

I'm what they call a Tropical Astrologer as I divide the year into seasons – but don't worry, we're going to learn the easy way to make a chart, and we'll leave the complicated stuff to someone else.

Astrology and astronomy were once the same science but they've now parted company. We still use astronomical data to calculate a birth chart, but the difference between astronomers and us is the *meaning* behind those planetary placements.

As Nicholas Campion says: 'Astrology's character descriptions constitute the world's oldest psychological model...which remains the most widely known form of personality analysis.'

So hopefully after you've read this little book, you'll understand not only how to satisfy a Taurus, but also its personality analysis and *why* being satisfied is so important to them.

Mary English
Bath, 2012

Chapter One

The Sign

Taurus is the second sign of the Zodiac and represented by 'the Bull'. The dates that generally relate to Taurus are 21st April to 21st May. I say 'generally' as it does depend where your Taurus was born and also what time of day.

As we divide the sky into 12 equal portions, our celestial divisions don't always line up with the way our calendar is calculated. As you might guess, the way the calendar divides the days doesn't match up totally with our orbit around the Sun, which is why we have leap years.

Astrology is about our orbit in space, and how the Sun looks to us from Earth – not about what might be written in a calendar – so sometimes the signs change quite late at night or early in the morning. All this data is recorded on the website we're going to use in the next chapter.

Each Sun sign of the Zodiac has a planet that looks after it. We call it their 'ruler'. The planet that rules Taurus is Venus and was originally called the Goddess Inanna by the Babylonians.

Goddess Inanna

The Goddess Inanna was an early version of what we in the West now call Venus. She was named after the planet that the Babylonians saw rising and falling in the sky.

Here's what Nick Campion has to say about Venus in his *The Dawn of Astrology*:

It oscillates between being a bright morning star, rising before the sun, and an equally striking evening star, appearing after dusk…Whether as morning or evening star, at its maximum distance from the sun, there are moments when Venus will briefly be the only visible star in the sky, dominating the heavens as a brilliant point of light. It is these periods that are separated by 584 days and five 584-day Venus cycles are completed in 8 years to the day, an observation which was recognised from the third millennium onwards in the use of an eight pointed star as Inanna's emblem.[2]

And here Diane Wolkstein (a Scorpio) talks about her origins in *Inanna, Queen of Heaven and Earth: Her Stories and Hymns from Sumer*.

Inanna's name means 'Queen of Heaven' and she was called both the First Daughter of the Moon and the Morning and Evening Star (the planet Venus). In addition, in Sumerian mythology, she was known as the Queen of Heaven and Earth and was responsible for the growth of plants and animals and fertility in humankind. Then, because of her journey to the underworld, she took on the powers and mysteries of death and rebirth.[3]

As Astrology progressed across the globe, it went via Rome and it was there that the name of the planet changed to Venus, and she's been called Venus ever since.

The Astronomy of Venus the Hot Planet

Venus is bright enough to be seen from the Earth with the naked eye. Like the Moon, it goes through phase changes, appearing as a bright light illuminated by the Sun, to a larger crescent, as it gets nearer to us, with some of it in shadow.

'Its surface is over twice as hot as your kitchen oven at 462 °C day and night. It is the closest planet to the Earth and similar in size.'[4]

Astronomers don't call the Moon a planet; they call it a satellite or celestial body...sounds rather dull to me, but in

Astrology we call *all* the bits we use 'planets', and sometimes astrologers call the Sun (which is technically a star) and the Moon 'lights' or 'luminaries': natural light-giving bodies.

Like the Earth, Venus is also made of rock but its climate has 'gone out of control'.[5]

It is surrounded by a dense layer of clouds and underneath these clouds the Russian probe 'Venera 7' landed on the surface in 1970 and discovered the extreme heat temperatures on the planet's surface. Other missions and probes sent back further information but it wasn't until 1990 that a US spacecraft called 'Magellan' orbited with cloud-penetrating radars and found out that the surface is totally dry with evidence of volcanic eruptions.

Every now and then Venus' orbit means it crosses over the Sun. Sort of like a mini-eclipse. It can't block out the Sun like the Moon can, as it's further away from us and only makes a black mark as you're looking at the Sun (which I don't recommend as that's dangerous to your eyes; you need to use special lenses).

This last happened in June 2004. The next visit will be in 2117, which is a bit of a long wait and I won't be around to see that!

Venus, the Goddess of Love

Venus salutes him with this fair good-morrow:
'O thou clear god, and patron of all light,
From whom each lamp and shining star doth borrow
The beauteous influence that makes him bright,
There lives a son that suck'd an earthly mother,
May lend thee light, as thou dost lend to other.'
Shakespeare, 'Venus and Adonis'[6]

When Astrology progressed across to Greece, the original Greek names for Venus were 'Herald of the Dawn' or 'Herald of Light' and sometimes 'Star of the Evening' because people saw it as visible early in the day and then as it orbited it became visible early in the evening. They eventually called her Aphrodite.

Then when Astrology made it to Rome they called her Venus, the Goddess of Love. She was the lover of Adonis, best mates with Eros the winged god and, just to complicate things, got caught in bed with Mars, even though she was married to the God Vulcan. Some things never change!

Astrology and Venus

Venus has hardly changed in meaning since the Babylonian times. Nicholas Campion tells us that in the 13th century talismans were made:

> A Venusian talisman, which might be made to enhance a love affair or soothe a fever, would have been made out of copper, Venus's metal, on Friday (Venus's day) after dawn (the first house on Friday was ruled by Venus), when Venus was in a sympathetic part of the zodiac, such as Taurus or Libra (the signs it ruled) and making good aspects to other planets. One talisman was made to ensure permanent love according to the following instructions:
>
> *'Make two talismans in an ascendant for good luck when the moon and Venus are in Taurus'*…as there are only a few days in the year when both Venus and the moon are both in Taurus, patience was required.[7]

This is a key word for Taurus: patience, but we will come on to that in a minute…

Colin Evans describes Venus as denoting 'the sense of beauty and the affections, love-life, artistic taste'.[8] These are also Taurus characteristics, especially the sense of beauty and artistic taste.

Other Astrologers' Views of Taurus

So what do other astrologers say about Taurus? How do they describe the characteristics of this sign?

Let's ask a living astrologer first, before we ask a few from the past.

Nina is an astrologer working and living in London in the UK. I asked her a few questions about her sign.

What makes you happy?

'Walks with my partner in the countryside, my allotment, harvesting and cooking, sharing a good meal with friends or family, delicious food, stroking and holding my cat, cuddles, doing needlework, looking at the stars, helping and looking after others, my work as an astrologer and hypnotherapist. These are not in order of importance although I guess the first two make me feel most connected to peace and joy.'

What is your definition of a good meal – price/taste/location – that type of thing?

'Delicious food in a cosy environment; food needs to be lovingly grown so I prefer restaurants which have meat that is free range, otherwise I'm a vegetarian.'

How important to you is your sex life (scale 1–10 with 10 being high and 1 low)?

'8.'

How do you feel when you break something or a possession gets damaged or goes missing? Please give me an example:

'I make really good friends with some items. I still wear clothes that I wore in my teens. I have no problem getting rid of things which are not useful. Items which I use, I'm very attached to. I often name appliances. This year we had to replace our dishwasher. We'd had it for 12 years. I had to say a proper goodbye and thanks for all its good

service and had a tear in the corner of my eye. It sounds daft but it looked after me for a long time! Worst was the loss of my laptop. I rely on my laptop for every aspect of my work. Communication, chart calculations, recording readings, editing and recording radio programmes, making hypnotherapy recordings for my clients, etc. To lose it was like losing my office. I haven't managed to get rid of it yet although I've become just as attached to my new one. It's my partner in my work!'

That seems very clear. Let's ask Colin Evans, editor of *The New Waites Compendium of Natal Astrology*, 1971:

Taurean individuals are practical, sure, plodding, secretive, reserved, fixed in purpose, possessing as a rule more vitality of mind and body than those born under any other sign. Extremely strong-willed, they can be led but never driven. They are the manufacturers, the builders, those who make and mould things. Taureans are averse to change, not very adaptable...[9]

Let's ask Caroline Casey in her *Making the Gods Work for You* in 1998:

As the bees buzz through the increasingly fragrant fields, Venus incarnates, making Taurus the most sensually intel-ligent of all the signs. Taste, texture, color, music – all nourish the Taurean, who knows that one can starve from aesthetic as well as caloric deprivation.[10]

That sounds a bit more balanced.

Let's ask Bil Teirney in his *All Around the Zodiac: Exploring Astrology's Twelve Signs*. He knows a thing or two about Taurus:

...the Bull's reputation as a slowpoke is exaggerated,

especially his 'slowness' is to be deemed undesirable (like a slow day at the office)...Taurus is a fixed-earth sign, suggesting a double dose of stability...Matter is appealingly solid and predictable to Taurus, a sign that needs to feel safely enclosed by protective and even permanent boundaries.[11]

Here's what Felix Lyle and Brian Aspland say in their book, *The Instant Astrologer*: 'Steadfast, patient, stable, methodical, deliberate, stubborn, productive, passive, restrained, affectionate, possessive, sensuous, self-indulgent, generous, grasping.'[12]

Quite a long list of attributes, going from positive to negative.

The saying 'Slow and steady wins the race' could have been coined to describe the Taurean approach to life. Quick and adaptable this sign may not be, but what it lacks in speed, it certainly makes up for in thoroughness, leaving few things to chance.

Here is Rae Orion in her *Astrology for Dummies*:

Concrete goals makes the most sense to you, and you pursue them with quiet persistence. Because you have an intense need for security, both emotional and financial, you tend to make cautious choices. Money is important to you, but you're also highly creative, and chances are you have talent in art or music.[13]

OK, we're having a bit more of an understanding about this sign. I think we should use the following keywords to describe Taurus accurately: Steady/Steadfast/Patient, Long-lasting/Permanent, Sensuous, Practical, Creative.

Steady/Steadfast/Patient

My dictionary defines 'steadfast' as: 'constant, firm and unwavering', and it is in these attributes that a Taurus excels. While a Gemini might change to learn more, or a Virgo might want to consider more than one option before they decide on something, a Taurus will tackle life in that firm and unwavering way. On the one hand it might seem boring or stuck-in-the-mud to other fast-paced signs, but on the other hand, without this ability to be steady the world would erupt in chaos. There has to be someone who is centred and 'earthed'.

Taurus Stevie Wonder wrote a song called 'Edge of Eternity' and there is a key line in it where he says that when the woman he loves is ready, 'holding strong and steady', he'll be there in her life, which describes very well a Taurean's commitment to wanting things to be steady.

Taureans also have an amazing capacity to wait for things. Truly wait. I have levels of patience rated at about minus 100, so I can't really understand the whole patience thing, but it is something that Taureans live by.

They will slowly and steadily work their way to the top of their profession or at least to a place where they feel comfortable. I even know Taureans who will baulk at promotion if they think things will change *too* much and they feel best where they are. Part of that steadiness is a fear of change.

Here's the Taurus actress Michelle Pfeiffer taking about her fears:

'I was kind of surprised to learn how controlling I am. I never thought of myself in that way. I think the root of the control issues is usually fear, because you want to know what's going to be happening at any given moment. So learning to accept and get comfortable with the unknown – I've got much better at that. I think children teach you that, too. Because you just can't control them – the more you try, the more you make matters worse. Having children has changed me more than anything.'

Nina tells us more about the slower side of life:

'I don't like the way that Taurus is often portrayed as stuck, materialistic and dull. This is a very creative sign. We take our pleasures from the slower side of life and value nurturing and the Earth. We could use more of these values in society, but I'm sure you already know that.'

Long-lasting/Permanent

To be happy, in a Taurus world, involves those things that don't change too much. Taureans can change, but they don't really like it, unless they've got planets in Gemini, Sagittarius or Virgo. They prefer things to stay. And that's not 'stay the same', just 'stay'.

So what does 'stay' mean?

Well, it's the opposite of 'go', surely?

My dictionary defines it as: 'remain in the same place'.

Now if you were an Air sign, or a Fire sign, the above description would have you running for the door. 'The same?' Argh!! An Aquarius would have departed years ago. However, to 'be the same' is to do what we're all rather bad at, which is just to 'be'.

We then get the definition: 'exist, take place, occupy a position in space, attend, consist of'.

There is not much to that, is there? Just to 'be'. I liked the phrase 'occupy a position in space', which is what astrologers have contemplated since the Babylonians…but which bit of space are you occupying? Where are you 'being'? How do you feel 'being' there? These aren't things that we as a species think about a lot (unless we're studying philosophy) but to 'be' is to act like a Taurus.

They don't question, like a Gemini might, what being is all about; they just 'are'.

And for something to last and not change it must just 'be'.

For more thoughts on this read *The Power of Now* by Eckhart Tolle. I always think it's fitting that an Aquarius should challenge the whole thought-process (which is what he does in the book) especially as he has Moon in Taurus…he wants to 'be' but has to question it…

For a Taurus, that ability to stay generally involves living at the same address, working in the same job, liking the same food or hobby.

Marla is a flower therapist, mother and medicine woman living and working in London, England. Healing isn't something she thought of as a career. It just happened naturally. She was introduced to Homeopathy and Flower Essences when she began Yoga to help with the birth of her first child. She found it worked really well. As a child, conventional medicine always disagreed with her. Her healing ability opened up after her first son was born. She met an Essence maker, who introduced her to her own gift.

She tells us how long she has lived at her present address:

'24 years, since I was in my late 20s.'

Famous Taurus psychoanalyst Sigmund Freud lived at the same address in Vienna Austria for 47 years and only moved out when the Nazis detained and interrogated his daughter Anna. He came to live in Hampstead, London, UK and (interestingly enough) *Freud's Vienna consulting room was recreated in faithful detail.*[14]

So not only did he manage to move house (change location) but all his important possessions came too and were laid out in exactly the same way as they'd been in Vienna. When I read that, I had a little chuckle!

Sensuous

There is no denying that the Earth-centred Taurus is in touch with their body and their sexuality. Ruled by Venus the Goddess of Love, their sensuousness is reflected in their need to experience love *through* their body, not because of it.

Here's Taurus Janet Jackson discussing what it's like to be

sensuous:

'Someone said to me, "Oh my God, you seem so quiet, and when I listen to your album it's so sensual," and I'm, like, "Well, am I supposed to be walking around with my butt hanging out and my boobs up to my ears, with voluptuous lips and high heels all the time?" That person still lives within me, but it doesn't necessarily mean it's there every single moment of the day.'

As she says, it's not something that's 'there' every moment of every day, but it is there.

The Taurus pop singer Adele confesses about her personal life:

'I am attentive. I will do anything for my man. I am a good cook. I'm funny. Always want to have sex. Well, most girls don't!'

Taurus Sigmund Freud spent his whole life analysing humans and came to this conclusion about sex and satisfaction:

'No one who has seen a baby sinking back satiated from the breast and falling asleep with flushed cheeks and a blissful smile can escape the reflection that this picture persists as a prototype of the expression of sexual satisfaction in later life.'

He believed it was innate and wired into us at birth.

Practical

To be is to do.
Immanuel Kant

One thing that a lot of astrologers miss when they describe the signs is that we actually live here on Earth, not up in the cosmos. And to successfully live on Earth, we have to use and utilise and make good use of our bodies and other practical things, otherwise we'd die. And one of those overreaching and important needs for our bodies is...food. There is no other way of approaching this.

I know this now, as I have just witnessed the passing away of a number of relatives. When someone is approaching death, the last thing they want to do is fill themselves with food. Just like when a baby is first born, it doesn't immediately need to eat. First of all it needs to get used to actually being in the world. Yes, it will want to suckle the mother's breast, but more importantly, it will want to feel warm and secure first.

So, when we're dying, that whole eating thing becomes a chore. Our appetite quite naturally leaves us, and we just want to be left, cosy and comfortable, without pain, in warm, dry, comforting surroundings, with people we love, who will care for us in our final moments.

It's only when we're well that we need to eat, to carry on living.

Someone who understood this more than most people was the very famous nurse Florence Nightingale. Not only was she a nurse, but she was a Taurus with Sun and Moon in that sign and so not only was she aware of bodily needs but she was also aware of the emotions surrounding food.

Food, Florence Nightingale and nursing

In her book on nursing, Florence spends a huge amount of space, quite correctly in my mind, devoted to eating and food:

TAKING FOOD
Want of attention to hours of taking food.

Every careful observer of the sick will agree in this that thousands of patients are annually starved in the midst of plenty, from want of attention to the ways which alone make it possible for them to take food. This want of attention is as remarkable in those who urge upon the sick to do what is quite impossible to them, as in the sick themselves who will not make the effort to do what is perfectly possible to them. For instance, to the large majority of very weak patients it is quite impossible to take any solid food before 11 A.M., nor then, if their strength is still further exhausted by fasting till that hour. For weak patients have generally feverish nights and, in the morning, dry mouths; and, if they could eat with those dry mouths, it would be the worse for them.

A spoonful of beef-tea, of arrowroot and wine, of egg flip, every hour, will give them the requisite nourishment, and prevent them from being too much exhausted to take at a later hour the solid food, which is necessary for their recovery. And every patient who can swallow at all can swallow these liquid things, if he chooses. But how often do we hear a mutton-chop, an egg, a bit of bacon, ordered to a patient for breakfast, to whom (as a moment's consideration would show us) it must be quite impossible to masticate such things at that hour. Again, a nurse is ordered to give a patient a tea-cup full of some article of food every three hours. The patient's stomach rejects it. If so, try a table-spoon full every hour; if this will not do, a tea-spoon full every quarter of an hour. I am bound to say, that I think more patients are lost by want of care and ingenuity in these momentous minutiae in private nursing than in public hospitals...[15]

No one could be more meticulous or have thought about a patient's diet more than a Taurus. Food and eating are almost a religion for them. They'll have certain knives or forks they like to use, certain cups they prefer to drink from, certain foods they prefer and ones that make their tummies upset or give them indigestion. If you're a therapist, or more especially if you're a homeopath, you can get to the correct remedy for your client if they're Taurus by asking them about their appetite, or the foods they like/dislike. It's a much easier way of getting to the centre of the case. If you ask more obvious questions, like 'How long has this been going on?', or 'Can you describe the pain?' they'll find it hard to answer them, but NO Taurus has ever found it difficult to describe their food requirements.

Food and emotion are also very linked

The Taurus novelist Anthony Trollope had a point when he said: *'Don't let love interfere with your appetite. It never does with mine.'*

As Taurus is the second sign of the Zodiac, we could look at it as Aries the first sign being about 'life and energy' while Taurus now brings us 'that which will sustain life', because without food, we wouldn't live long at all.

I'll tell you a little story. I know a young Gemini man whose mother is Taurus. He went overseas to university. On his first few weeks there, he was so excited and scared and consumed by the difference of it all and equally our rotten weather here in the UK, that after a while he stopped eating and his girlfriend got very worried (understandably). Had he been at home, his mother would have fussed all over him. As he'd never had to truly care for himself before, this little exercise in stimulating his mind, but not looking after his (rather important) body, resulted in him becoming extremely unwell and taking to his bed. He blamed the weather. His focus was on his mind. His mother's (and his girlfriend's) was on his body. No one was right or wrong, but a Taurus away from home for the first time is unlikely to starve!

Marla (whom we met earlier) tells us her views on eating:

'I'm not so concerned about glittering surroundings so long as the food is good. It could be Chinese, Indian, fish and chips or steak and chips with veg. So long as it's cooked well and not mean with the portions. I don't like nouvelle cuisine. Small portions displayed like a piece of artwork on a plate don't interest me. Give me a decent portion any day, or why am I bothering to eat?!!!

It could be a £5 fish and chips takeaway, or a meal in a restaurant (nice, so I don't have to wash up)! But I personally won't pay more than about £15–20, unless someone else is offering! Not keen on complicated mixtures or flavours and spices. Some of which I just can't eat as my stomach won't let me. However, recently I was taken to a lovely, posh, but not too OTT restaurant in the States (a steak house). I really enjoyed the opportunity to dress up and be treated for a change.'

In this little example, Marla's views of food changed when she was taken out and someone else was paying (!)...and the emphasis was on enjoyment and the company, not just on the food itself.

Caroline is an author and also a holistic therapist (I meet a lot of therapists in my line of work!). Here are her favourite types of food:

'Home-cooked by me...Sunday roast. Going out...Italian or good Scottish ethically sourced. Love really nice restaurants and will pay extra as a treat to go to Michelin-starred places and eat amazing food. Hate fast food and being ripped off. I wish I didn't love food so much as I am much too fat. I hate cheap ice cream...must be the real McCoy. Same with coffee. I like to bake and cook.'

I can attest to these points, as my husband is a Taurus. If we go out to eat and the portions are small, it doesn't matter how wonderfully it is presented, he just feels short-changed. Also if 'normal' food is really expensive, again he feels ripped off.

One evening we went to a local restaurant we'd never been to before. It's always packed, no spare seats, and every day it's open it is full. The chef must be a Taurus.

Even though the food is expensive – not wildly so, but more than you'd pay normally – he comes to the table and tells you what he's made and *why*. The kitchen is open-plan so you can see him prepare each course (there are lots) and his food is more of a live art/theatre-event than a traditional meal. My husband wasn't worried by any of this and was fascinated about each course. The flavours were lovely and tasty, and even though each course was small, after eating 5 or 6 we were soon full up! Even the desserts were lovingly hand-prepared and, since I'm a vegan, the chef had gone to the trouble to source vegan-friendly ingredients, so everyone was happy.

One thing is for sure. If you eat out with a Taurus, don't expect scintillating conversation. Leave that to the Geminis.

My ex-husband, who is Gemini, took me out to eat almost every weekend when we first met. Each week we'd go somewhere different. He wasn't concerned with portion size, or ingredients, and one of the places we went to was an East End chippie where we had eels and mash with a weird green sauce called 'eel liquor sauce' made with parsley.

What he wanted to do was amaze me with his knowledge of these *different* locations. The food was just a backdrop to this desire to entertain me, and we had a little joke about how he'd wooed me over an Indian meal. He even, later, made a funny cartoon strip out of this, with photos of us eating. He does have Moon in Taurus, but his Gemini Sun wanted to entertain.

It's different for a Taurus. Eating is *serious* and they want to eat, not chat, at mealtimes. This was a surprise for me when my Taurus and I were dating, as our family mealtimes (my family are mostly Air and Fire) revolved around 'big' discussions about Life, the Universe and Everything...with arguments and excitement and siblings hogging the conversation. The only quiet one was my Earth sign sister. She just wanted to eat, not chat! So when our mealtimes were quiet affairs, I almost missed that family repartee, until I realised that the time to chat with a Taurus is when nothing else is happening. And NOT when you're eating...

Celia is an author, mother, wife, writer, gardener and spiritual teacher.

She tells us about her views on food:

'Organic; mostly veggies, a soup or stir-fry. Also fish and chips! All best at home.'

Again the emphasis is on 'comfort' and 'home'.

Creative

The painting rises from the brushstrokes as a poem rises from the words. The meaning comes later.
Artist Joan Miro

One thing that is hardly featured when astrologers write about Taurus is their love of creativity. I know countless Taurus artists, who are so modest about their ability. I read for a Taurus lady once whose husband was also an artist, and we heard far more about *his* work than hers (he was a Leo), so next time they visited, I asked her to bring some of her work over. It was lovely. Soft colours, beautiful shapes, gentle on the eye. They both taught art at their local college but Mrs Taurus lived for her creations.

I won't list the numbers of Taurus artists, but just take my word for it, there are plenty. The Taurus friends I now have, including my husband, are artists of one form or another.

Famous Renaissance painter Leonardo da Vinci had some very strong views on art.

And if you, O poet, tell a story with your pen, the painter with his brush can tell it more easily, with simpler completeness and less tedious to be understood. And if you call painting dumb poetry, the painter may call poetry blind painting. Now which is the worse defect? to be blind or dumb? Though the poet is as free as the painter in the invention of his fictions they are not so satisfactory to men as paintings; for, though poetry is able to describe forms, actions and places in words, the painter deals with the actual similitude of the forms, in order to represent them. Now tell me which is the nearer to the actual man: the name of man or the image of the man. The name of man differs in different countries, but his form is never changed but by death.[16]

There is a British artist called David Shepherd, who is famous for his wildlife paintings. He explained how he would have become a bus driver, when he was turned down by an art school: 'I tried to get into the Slade School of Fine Art and they looked at my work and said "go and drive a bus."'[17] Luckily he met a painter called Robin Goodwin at a cocktail party who agreed to take him on as an apprentice. I wonder if they knew that they are the same Sun sign? Both of them are Taurus.

David's interviewer, Vivienne, tells us how practical and down-to-earth this training was:

David is known for his strong work ethic, something impressed upon him by his mentor Robin Goodwin who not only taught his apprentice how to paint but also about the commercial aspects of a career in art, pointing out to him that in order to pay the bills he would need to work eight hour days, seven days a week.[17]

Interesting how not only did the painting satisfy the creative side of the Taurus Sun, but also the practical side, as without money, life is exceedingly difficult.

Chapter Two

How to Make a Chart

These days, making a chart is simple. In the 'old days' you would have needed to have a really good knowledge of mathematics, the ability to calculate long complicated degrees and angles, and access to the tables of planetary positions we call the Ephemeris.

You would then have to work out which sign was 'Rising' or 'Ascending' over the horizon and place it all into a circle, taking into account the fact that birth times and places throughout the world vary... not forgetting things like 'Summer Time' or 'War Time'. The advent of computers has reduced all of that calculation and hard work down to sometimes seconds rather than days.

Not that making something quicker makes it better, but you can get a computer program to do just about anything, provided the person who wrote the program knows what they're doing.

We're going to use a Swiss website called http://www.astro.com.

Obviously, being Swiss makes it all the more accurate and it's also a website that astrologers use, so you'll be in safe hands.

Equal House System

Make yourself an account, and then go to the part of the site called 'Extended Chart Selection'. In this section of their website, halfway down the page is a section called 'Options' and underneath it says: 'House System', and if you look at it now it will say 'default'.

Click in this box and change it to 'equal' so that the segments of the chart which we call 'houses' are all the same size.

Now click the blue button on the right that says: 'click here to show the chart'.

You will now be taken to another page on the site that will have your Taurus' birth chart. It will look something like the chart in the next chapter.

There will be a circle with the symbols for the signs of the Zodiac on the outside of the circle, the circle divided into 12 equal portions (houses), and if you look carefully you will see the symbol for the Sun ☉ and the Moon ☽.

The houses are numbered 1–12 in an anti-clockwise order.

These are the shapes representing the signs, so find the one that matches yours. They are called 'glyphs':

Aries ♈
Taurus ♉
Gemini ♊
Cancer ♋
Leo ♌
Virgo ♍
Libra ♎
Scorpio ♏
Sagittarius ♐
Capricorn ♑
Aquarius ♒
Pisces ♓

The Elements

To understand your Taurus fully, you must take into account which element their Ascendant and Moon are in.

Each sign of the Zodiac has been given an element that it operates under: Earth, Air, Fire, and Water. I like to think of them as operating at different 'speeds'.

The **Earth** signs are our friend **Taurus**, **Virgo** and **Capricorn**. The Earth element is stable, grounded and concerned with practical matters. A Taurus with a lot of Earth in their chart works best at a very slow, steady speed. (I refer to these in the text as 'Earthy'.)

The **Air** signs are **Gemini, Libra** and **Aquarius** (who is the 'Water-carrier', *not* a Water sign). The Air element enjoys ideas, concepts and thoughts. It operates at a faster speed than Earth, not as fast as Fire but faster than Water and Earth. Imagine them as being medium speed.

The **Fire** signs are **Aries, Leo** and **Sagittarius**. The Fire element likes action, excitement and can be very impatient. Their speed is *very* fast. (I refer to these as Firey i.e. Fire-sign.)

The **Water** signs are **Cancer, Scorpio** and **Pisces**. The Water element involves feelings, impressions, hunches and intuition. They operate faster than Earth but not as fast as Air. A sort of slow-medium speed.

Chapter Three

The Ascendant

Name: ♀ Queen of England Elizabeth II			
born on We., 21 April 1926	Time:	2:40 a.m.	ASTRO DIENST
in London, ENG (UK)	Univ.Time:	1:40	www.astro.com
0w10, 51n30	Sid. Time:	15:32:50	Type: 2.GW 0.0-1 4-Nov-2012

Natal Chart (Method: Web Style / equal)
Sun sign: Taurus
Ascendant: Capricorn

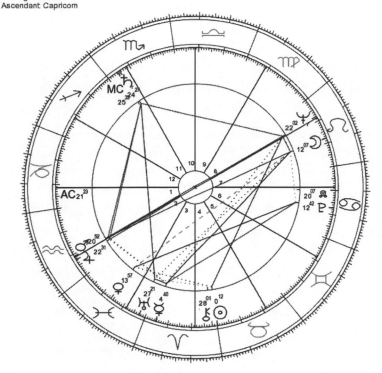

In our chart example, Elizabeth has a Capricorn Ascendant. If
you look at the chart above, you will see the initials AC and the
numbers 21 on the left-hand side of the chart.

The AC is in the centre of the section in the circumference of
the circle that has got the Capricorn symbol, which looks like the
number 7 with a blob on it.

This is Astro-Speak for 'Elizabeth has her Ascendant at 21

degrees of Capricorn'. (There are 30 degrees to each sign, x 12 signs = 360 degrees.)

In Astrology we classify the Ascendant as being the outside part of you, the bit that people meet first. The image we want people to see, in fact the image people *will* see.

Your Ascendant is what you display at a party, or to your parents, or when you're under pressure. It's the coat you wear, the glasses you see the world through, how you viewed the world when you came into it.

Your Beginning

As you were being born, the Sun was in one sign, the Moon and all the planets were in other signs, and *the* most important part of your chart was in a sign signifying how you 'came into the world'.

It could be in the sign of Gemini, making your Taurus chatty and friendly. The Air sign speeds the energies up and makes the person more likely to take things at a faster pace than say someone with a slower Earth Asc, who will take…their…time…and…do…things…more…slowly. Or it could have been in the sign of Cancer, wanting to 'feel at home', loving Mum, wanting protection and financial security.

Someone who has a Firey Ascendant will be more proactive, more of a 'doing' sort than someone with a Water Ascendant, who will want to wait, be slower, *feel* their way into a situation.

Understanding the Ascendant explains your Taurus' first breath, how they first saw the world as a baby, and it's an important part of a chart.

But what if your Taurus is adopted, or their parents have died, or they were born during a blackout or a power cut?

Then you have to remember that it will be difficult, not impossible, to make a correct chart. If you know the date, then that at least is a starting point, but for the purposes of this book, you need date, time, location.

Now that you know what Ascendant your Taurus has, here are the 12 Ascendant signs so you can read the one that matches the chart you have made. Your Taurus is still a Taurus, but the way they project themselves will be because of their Ascndant sign.

Aries Ascendant

I focus on the writing and let the rest of the process take care of itself. I've learned to trust my own instincts and I've also learned to take risks.
Sue Grafton

Aries is a Fire sign, the first sign of the Zodiac, and as such, needs to *be* 'first'. They are likened to a baby that wants attention, so a Taurus with Aries Ascendant will always want to lead and to be first in the queue. They won't want to wait for anyone or anything and might be a bit impatient (all the Fire signs are). They are more proactive, more brave and more assertive.

Taurus Ascendant

You simply have to put one foot in front of the other and keep going. Put blinders on and plough right ahead.
George Lucas

Taurus is an Earth sign, and gives a grounded approach. For a Taurus to have this Ascendant doubles all those Taurus things we discussed earlier. It means they'll remember to have lunch, remember to look after their bodies, and be happy with a more simple life. However, their finances can be an issue and they might fret about their bank balance.

Gemini Ascendant

I had a big mouth, and I used to mouth off to my mother all the time. But I'd make sure my father wasn't in earshot, because he'd let me have it.
Michelle Pfeiffer

Gemini is an Air sign and involves communication and change, and a Taurus with this Asc might move house (relocate) a lot, be on the phone 24/7, love change and conversation, and be capable of communicating with anyone, anywhere. They're good at asking questions, good at enquiring about issues, maybe not so good at staying the course if things get tricky. *Vive la Différence* should be their call sign.

Cancer Ascendant

Every time a child says 'I don't believe in fairies' there is a little fairy somewhere that falls down dead.
James M. Barrie

Cancer is a Water sign, the sign of the home and family, and this is a nice sign for a Taurus to have as it complements their Sun sign. Provided this combination has been mothered and cared for in a gentle way when young, they can grow to be quite confident individuals. They will love home-cooking and all aspects of family life.

Leo Ascendant

My weaknesses...I wish I could come up with something. I'd probably have the same pause if you asked me what my strengths are. Maybe they're the same thing.
Al Pacino

Leo is another Fire sign and adds regality and a nice strong exterior for a Taurus. They expect the red carpet to be rolled out for them and like their egos to be stroked. Underneath this flashy-loving exterior will be the Taurus Sun, still practical, still down to earth. They're good in a crisis, as the Fire element will send them in bravely where other signs might fear to tread.

Virgo Ascendant

If you're somebody like me, and there's millions of us out there who are interested in astrology, meditation, numerology, feng shui, aging, good health, women's health…
Shirley MacLaine

Virgo is an Earth sign and brings a practical approach to life. Virgo Asc wants a place for everything and everything in its place. They will want to be able to analyse things, explain things and have reasons for Life, the Universe and Everything. They can also fret more than normal about their health. They need things to be 'ordered' and 'organised'.

Libra Ascendant

You never really understand a person until you consider things from his point of view.
Harper Lee

Libra is an Air sign and as represented by the scales needs to feel balanced. With this combination, a Taurus will put a lot of energy into their personal love life, their partners and close relationships. Libra Asc also *hates* arguments and people falling out so will do anything to avoid clashes. They like to be surrounded by pleasing decorations, pastel colours, anything as long as it is beautiful, as Libra is also 'ruled' by Venus, the

Goddess of Love.

Scorpio Ascendant

He that has eyes to see and ears to hear may convince himself that no mortal can keep a secret. If his lips are silent, he chatters with his fingertips; betrayal oozes out of him at every pore.
Sigmund Freud

Scorpio is another Water sign, intense and deep, and usually in a crowd or company will appear quiet and withdrawn. It's a strong Asc for a Taurus to have and can tend towards suspicion at the worst and transformation at the best. They look at life through glasses that peer deep into people's souls, as they focus intently on their goals. Make sure you don't get on the wrong side of this Asc – because the backlash can be severe. On the positive side, they are great achievers.

Sagittarius Ascendant

The noblest pleasure is the joy of understanding.
Leonardo da Vinci

Sagittarius is another Fire sign and wants to travel, be free, philosophise, learn, teach and be in foreign cultures. As long as there are no ties and plenty of rope, Sag Asc will generally look at life in a positive, upbeat and happy manner. This is quite a cheerful Asc and helps a Taurus see the better side of life. They love to debate and instil their knowledge into the collective conciousness.

Capricorn Ascendant

There is no better teacher than adversity. Every defeat, every heart-break, every loss, contains its own seed, its own lesson on how to improve your performance next time.
Malcolm X

Capricorn is another Earth sign and, ruled by Saturn, makes a challenging Asc for a Taurus because it can make the individual negative and always fearing the worst. The plus side is that life gets better as they get older, as they learn that age and experience are valuable assets. It does makes a Taurus doubly sensible and they may be drawn to have friends that are older than them.

Aquarius Ascendant

Necessity is blind until it becomes conscious. Freedom is the consciousness of necessity.
Karl Marx

Aquarius is an Air sign, ruled by wacky Uranus, the planet of rebellion. Their deep desire is for friendship and they want to be friends with everybody. Not just chummy friends but friends they can play with, do interesting things with, and be part of something bigger like 'Save the Earth'. It can make them a little colder than other combinations, but on the plus side, their diaries are full and their Xmas card list, long.

Pisces Ascendant

I believe God rules all by his divine providence and that the stars by his permission are instruments.
William Lilly

Pisces Ascendant can be drawn into addictions and dependencies and feel empathy to everyone's hard-luck story. If your child or partner has this combination, they need space on their own, gentle handling, and lots of time dreaming and sleeping. They love the mystical, the unexplained and that which cannot be described in words. Intuition is a given.

Chapter Four

The Moon

The conscious mind may be compared to a fountain playing in the sun and falling back into the great subterranean pool of subconscious from which it rises.
Sigmund Freud

The Moon in Astrology represents how we feel about things. If the Sun is who we are, and the Ascendant is how we project ourselves, then the Moon is how we respond emotionally.

In reality the Moon reflects the light of the Sun, so astrologers describe it in the same way: that the sign of the Moon reflects how we feel.

The difference between a thought and a feeling is this: A thought is something that happens swiftly and comes from our minds. A feeling happens just after the thought and comes from our heart.

If you hit me, I might think, 'Crikey, why did he do *that*?' Then the feeling of pain in my jaw would follow, then the emotion of sadness or anger, depending on how my chart is constructed. But in any given situation, there will be a thought, then an emotion, and that emotion is the Moon.

In reality the Moon changes sign every two days or so. If you ever want to do an interesting experiment, read the headlines of the daily papers and pay attention to the Moon signs.

On an Aries Moon day, more people are fighting; on a Cancer Moon day, more about the home; on a Pisces Moon day, there might be news about weird and wonderful and inexplicable mysteries. Try it – you'll be surprised.

Getting in touch with our Moon signs is a very useful exercise. You know how it is, you want to leave your job and you hate your boss, and your Sun in Sagittarius is happy to leave. But have you run this past your Moon in Capricorn, that is worried you'll never get another job and will become penniless? So all that happens is, you keep saying you want to do something but it never happens. Your concious self is perfectly happy about these changes, but your subconcious self is worrying and can easily sabotage your actions. For more thoughts on this, read anything by Sigmund Freud.

I recommend, if you're stuck somewhere in your life, find out the sign of your Moon and have a little chat with it and see if it's happy to do what you want. The subconcious is like a child and believes everything it's told. The Bach Flower Essences help the Moon to feel less scared and worried. I use them a lot in my private practice.

The Dr Bach Flower Essences

In 1933 Dr Edward Bach, a medical doctor and homeopath, published a little booklet called *The Twelve Healers and Other Remedies*. His theory was that if the emotional component a person was suffering from was removed, their 'illness' would also disappear. I tend to agree with this kind of thinking as most illnesses (except being hit by a bus) are preceded by an unhappy event or an emotional disruption that then sets into place the body getting out of sync. Removing the emotional issue and bringing a bit of stability into someone's life, when they are having a hard time, can improve their overall health so much that wellness resumes.

Knowing which Bach Flower Essence can help certain worries and upsetments gives you and your Taurus more control over your lives. I recommend the Essences a lot in my practice if I feel a certain part of a person's chart is under stress...and usually it's the Moon that needs help. The Essences describe the negative aspects of the character, which are focused on during treatment. This awareness helps reverse those trends, so when our emotional selves are nice and comfortable, we can then face each day with more strength.

I've quoted Dr Bach's actual words for each sign.

To use the Essences take 2 drops from the stock bottle and put them into a glass of water and sip. I tend to recommend putting them into a small water bottle and sipping them throughout the day, at least 4 times. For young children, do the same.

Remember to seek medical attention if symptoms don't get better and/or seek professional counselling.

Aries Moon

If you don't ask, you don't get.
Stevie Wonder

An Aries Moon will want all their needs met, loved for who they are and for what they do, as Aries is an action sign. They feel better having everything they need, right here, right now. Patience won't wash. Aries Moon processes their emotions by action, lots of it. Running, jumping, physical expression is good but, however their Moon operates, it will be swift, fast and immediate. Like a storm, it will all seem very spectacular and invigorating, then in a few moments the storm will pass, and they'll be back to their friendly selves. Their feelings are expressed powerfully and impetuously, and they may find it hard to distance themselves from them. The most obvious benefit of this is the honesty of their gut reaction to events.

Bach Flower Essence Impatiens: *'Those who are quick in thought and action and who wish all things to be done without hesitation or delay.'*

Taurus Moon

*My greatest strength is common sense. I'm really a standard brand
– like Campbell's tomato soup or Baker's chocolate.*
Katharine Hepburn

Taurus Moon will need their emotional needs to be met by
sensuality, fine food, fine wine, luxurious silks and satins. Their
Moon is slower, and takes time to respond. They feel through
having their bellies filled and their finances stable. A good meal
and a cheque from the boss will calm most Taurus Moon fears.
Taurean fixity makes them an emotionally consistent person,
slow to change their heart. In a crisis some Taurus Moons will not
be able to *do* anything. They have to stop and think and 'let it all
sink in'. If their steady, slow progress is interrupted by some
obstacle, they get down-hearted and discouraged.

Bach Flower Essence Gentian: *'Those who are easily discouraged.
They may be progressing well in the affairs of their daily life, but any
small delay or hindrance to progress causes doubt and soon disheartens
them.'*

Gemini Moon

As with anything creative, change is inevitable.
Enya

Oh Gemini Moon, they're not so easy to placate! As long as they
have 15 different people to discuss their issues with, 12 self-help
books and a focus for their changeable emotions, they're fine.
Gemini is an airy, abstract energy and they are likely to analyse
and rationalise their emotions more than the average. The plus
side of this is the clarity of self-knowledge; the minus is that they
may end up simply worrying about it all too much. Sometimes
the answer to the problem may be to simply turn off the brain for

a while. One thing is for sure, during an emotional crisis, the Gemini Moon's phone bill goes through the roof.

This Essence comes under the heading 'For Those Who Suffer Uncertainty' (which Libra and Gemini both suffer from).

Bach Flower Essence Cerato: *'Those who have not sufficient confidence in themselves to make their own decisions.'*

Cancer Moon

Perhaps it is a good exercise to work out what we would say to our children if we knew we were about to die.
David Servan-Schreiber

As the sign Cancer is 'ruled' by the Moon, their emotional self is happy in this sign. They might find their emotions are very influenced by the sign the Moon is in during the week, so get a good Moon calendar and pay attention to what sign the Moon is in. Cancer is a Water sign and can hold onto emotions they should have let go of years ago, but overall it makes them extra-sensitive to others' emotional needs. This is a highly 'maternal' influence making their emotions well tuned into protecting and nurturing others. It also greatly increases sensitivity, so bear in mind that a Taurus with a Cancer Moon needs their emotions to be carefully taken into consideration.

Bach Flower Essence Clematis: *'Living in the hopes of happier times, when their ideals may come true.'*

Leo Moon

Why am I so famous? What am I doing right? What are the others doing wrong?'
Barbra Streisand

Leo Moon is a contradiction for a Taurus. A Moon that wants

recognition, when the Sun really wants to be in the background. Their emotional needs are best met when someone can recognise their need to feel thanked and respected and most of all praised. They have the ability to react swiftly to emotional situations and as a 'fixed' Fire sign feel best having special moments and 'me time'. Red carpets wouldn't be amiss either as Leo's traditional love of being in the limelight means that Moon-in-Leo people are likely to have an instinct for being the centre of attention.

Bach Flower Essence Vervain: *'Those with fixed principles and ideas, which they are confident are right.'*

Virgo Moon

The problem wasn't the booze; it was the fact that it no longer worked as a medicine to fix the dire consequences of my self-obsession, overwork, selfishness and manic depression.
Pete Townshend

Virgo Moon's challenge is to *not* fret about things, *not* worry themselves to a frenzy and learn to trust that everything will work out OK. Virgo Moons are good at absorbing feelings and rationalising them.Their only problem is when there is too much to deal with; then they become like a rabbit frozen in the headlights. Virgo Moons are often seen as somewhat challenging because Virgo wants order and harmony and this sits uncomfortably with our notoriously uncontrollable emotions.

This is my most often prescribed remedy, as Virgo Moon, Sun, Asc are my best customers. It comes under the heading 'Over-Sensitive to Influences and Ideas'.

Bach Flower Essence Centaury: *'Their good nature leads them to do more than their own share of work and they may neglect their own mission in life.'*

Libra Moon

I believe in love that's fun, that is caring, giving, and that is honest.
Jordan Knight

A Taurus with a Libra Moon does need people. Friendly, loving people that don't argue or swear. They love beauty and shades of pastel, and as long as they can connect with others who can appreciate their gentle genteelness, they're fine. How everyone gets on with everyone else is a major concern, and their partner will, if they're not careful, become a major focus in life. On a down day they have problems making up their mind and can sway from one idea to another as Libran energy puts a strong emphasis on harmony and balance. They also long for a partner and would rather be in a bad relationship than not in one at all.

Bach Flower Essence Scleranthus: *'Those who suffer from being unable to decide between two things, first one seeming right then the other.'*

Scorpio Moon

U2 is an original species...there are colours and feelings and emotional terrain that we occupy that is ours and ours alone.
Bono

Scorpio is a strong Moon and one that can absorb a large amount of negative energy without falling apart. Their feelings are intense, fixed and deep. Their emotional needs are not light and fluffy as they reside somewhere deep like a cavern or underground volcano. They can be tense and if they want something, by hook or by crook, they'll get it. Consequently, when things don't go to plan, a Moon in Scorpio will project all their disappointments onto the outside world. I don't often see this combination as most of the time they can manage in life and are quite self-sufficient. Trust is extremely important to them. If you want someone to help the underdog this is the sign combination that is wonderful for that.

This Essence comes under the heading 'Over-Care for Welfare Of Others.'

Bach Flower Essence Chicory: *'They are continually correcting what they consider wrong and enjoy doing so.'*

Sagittarius Moon

It's been a long journey.
Andy Murray

Sagittarius Moon makes for quite an unusual combination. Sagittarius is so famed for putting their foot in their mouth and saying what others only think, while Taurus is the sign of doing the practical stuff. So there their Moon is: wanting answers and reasons and a nice long trip to Outer Mongolia, friendly, sociable and philosophical. It is ruled by upbeat, benevolent Jupiter and usually gives a trusting and positive outlook on life and people. Moon-in-Sagittarius people always bounce back and never lose their fundamental faith in humanity.

This Essence comes under the heading 'Over-Sensitive to Influences and Ideas'. Reading something upsetting will influence them a great deal.

Bach Flower Essence Agrimony: *'They hide their cares behind their humour and jesting and try to bear their trials with cheerfulness.'*

Capricorn Moon

I take that part of my life very seriously. I want to be a successful businessman. It's as simple as that.
David Beckham

Of all the Moon signs, Capricorn is probably the most challenging. It is ruled by scary Saturn, the grim reaper and planet of hard knocks, so their emotional make-up is severe and self-flagillating. Like Scorpio Moon they can absorb more negativity than other signs but it makes them fearful of more pain. 'Stop beating yourself up' would be a good motto. Capricorn, more than any other sign, recognises the tough material reality of the world, while the Moon is the 'inner child', and may not feel at all at home in this strict environment.

Bach Flower Essence Mimulus: *'Fear of worldly things, illness, pain, accident, poverty, of dark, of being alone, of misfortune. They secretly bear their dread and do not speak freely of it to others.'*

Aquarius Moon

We're born alone, we live alone, we die alone. Only through our love and friendship can we create the illusion for the moment that we're not alone.
Orson Welles

That Aquarius flavour can make a Taurus *so* detached from their emotions. Air signs don't do emotions very well; they prefer to think rather than feel and can become overwhelmed if there is too much emotion around. They may find their emotions hard to deal with as Aquarian energy is airy and gives them a natural tendency to consider them in an abstract way. Equally, it is a fixed energy, and emotions are famously fluid and hard to pin down. The result is they are very unlikely to wear their heart on their sleeve and may seem cool and unpredictable.

Bach Flower Essence Water Violet: *'For those who like to be alone, very independent, capable and self-reliant. They are aloof and go their own way.'*

Pisces Moon

Why does the eye see a thing more clearly in dreams than the imagination when awake?
Leonard da Vinci

If you're involved with a Pisces Moon, take a deep breath. This makes for an especially sensitive soul. They'll certainly be creative, musical, inspired, talented, *but* they might not know what day of the week it is, where they put their watch, wallet, money or bus fare. If they are cared for in a Steiner-type environment that takes this gentleness into account, they will do well. As Pisces is the most emotional of the signs, they have access to acute emotional sensitivity, which makes life complicated, and action difficult. This is the sign of the martyr and they have an awareness of life's suffering. Moon-in-Pisces is often seen as a combination giving mystical insight, so they might also have a natural psychic or intuitive side.

This Essence comes under the heading 'For Those Who Have Fear' and will help this fragile, gentle soul take courage to face any emergency, be it the death of a beloved pet, starting school, getting a new job or starting a new relationship.

Bach Flower Essence Rock Rose: *'For cases where there even appears no hope or when the person is very frightened or terrified.'*

Chapter Five

The Houses

This is one part of Astrology that most people get the most confused about. What is a 'house'?

It's a mathematical division of the circle. The Ascendant, as we have learned, is deduced by the time of birth. It isn't an actual place or planet; it's a time location. The houses are the segments of the circle which we have created, then divided into 12. A bit like pieces of a pizza.

Astrologers haven't always made charts in a circle; they've also been made into squares. But if you ask me, a circle seems to make more sense, otherwise you miss the lovely shapes that the planets can make around the circle, which is one of my passions. I love the shapes that charts make and spent five years researching the birth charts of Indigo children. More information on this link: http://www.maryenglish.com/indigo1.html.

One thing is for sure, a birth chart does represent the position of the planets, on the day of birth, in the sky. But I know a lot of people who look at a chart and wonder what the hell it all *means*.

So, a house is a segment of that circle. The centre of the circle represents the Earth, and each segment represents a different 'area' of life. Those areas range from how others see you, to how you see yourself and everything in between.

I suppose when the original astrologers had made their little maps of the heavens, they must have thought: 'Having the Sun in the 4th section must be different from having it in the 8th.' Astrologers have argued for long enough, over the years, as to which 'system' of division works the best, so we can't really say that each house is something real.

House Systems

Now, just to make things complicated, there are about 5 or more house 'systems' that are used. The most popular one in all the computer programs is called 'Placidus', but that is only because most books are written using it. It wasn't actually used in the UK until the 18th century. It's the default system on the astro.com website.

The 'system' used *before* this is the Equal House System, the one that I prefer and really enjoy using. The Equal House System uses the Ascendant as the 1st cusp and then divides the whole Zodiac into 12 equal parts for the 12 'houses'.

The Placidus system takes into account far more complicated data and means each 'house' of the chart is a different size.

'Why make things complicated?' is my question. Life is complicated enough already, which is why I use the Equal House System. If you're using a computer program or an Internet site, please check which system is being used and change it to Equal House.

Easy!

The Sun can 'fall' into any house, depending on the time of birth. So here are the 12 houses you can have in your chart. Look to see which house the Sun has appeared and read the interpretation for that. In our chart example, the Queen has her Sun in her 4th house.

The First House: House of Personality

Know your power.
Jordan Knight

The first house comes straight after the Ascendant and is almost *the* most important house and is just as significant as the Sun or Moon signs. Temperament, personality, health are all expressed here; it is the 'character' of the person. If your Taurus has their

Sun here, they will be more forceful, more confident and generally more self-assured.

The Second House: House of Money, Material Possessions and Self-Worth

Don't hunt for deer in pig country.
Barry Crump

The second house rules our first relations with the outer world. It covers material things, money and possessions, security and stability. If these sound like Taurus keywords, that's because each house from 1 to 12 is a little like each sign of the Zodiac, and the 2nd house is like Taurus. It's the balance between the attitude to material goods (e.g. hard cash) and spiritual goods such as love and friends and also the sense of self-worth. A Taurus with their Sun here will be more inclined to focus on their finances before they can do more fluffy stuff.

The Third House: House of Communication and Short Journeys

I hope this dedicated epistle of mine published without your knowledge, shall…find easy remission at your most gentle hands.
William Lilly

This house rules learning to speak and think, and relations with close relatives, especially brothers and sisters. There is also a connection with the mind, which means that planetary influences here in the third house may well make the individual liable to change their mind a lot. They will love all forms of communication, will have more than one phone, like texting, love to stay in touch with others and will especially enjoy short, local journeys. Keeping mentally 'on the move' is a must.

The Fourth House: House of Home, Family and Roots

Like all best families, we have our share of eccentricities, of impetuous and wayward youngsters and of family disagreements.
Queen Elizabeth II

The fourth house covers the home and domestic life in general and is influenced by home-loving qualities. This house also describes relations with the mother or maternal figure, but it is also seen as the attitude to both parents, and to 'roots' in general, wherever or whatever they are. They will enjoy all home comforts, love being at home, cooking and keeping house. They enjoy all forms of family get-togethers and can be sentimental and animal loving.

The Fifth House: House of Creativity and Romance

The painter who draws merely by practice and by eye, without any reason, is like a mirror which copies every thing placed in front of it without being conscious of their existence.
Leonardo da Vinci

The fifth house covers the development of the desire to make a mark in the wider world. What exactly this 'wider world' is, very much depends upon the individual. It could be anything creative or active 'out there' – cooking, playing, art, creativity, love affairs, gambling or partying. This is the house that is concerned with creation and includes giving birth to children or creative ideas. They also love being the centre of attention.

The Sixth House: House of Work and Health

Not so this figment! – not, that such a fume,
Instead of giving way to time and health,
Should eat itself into the life of life.
Robert Browning

The sixth house is the development of organisation and discipline, tidiness and/or the ability to be organised. The influence of practicality and personal health is featured in this house. The Taurus Sun in the 6th does need to be organised but not at the expense of sanity or comfortableness. The 6th house governs health and what work we do, and I've found clients with this placement are happiest when they have a caring or health-based job or do volunteer work assisting others.

The Seventh House: House of Relationships and Marriage

There's never been a day of doubt ever since that I'm with the right person.
Joanna Lumley

The seventh house is the first of the houses which really turns from the 'inner' concerns of the individual, psychological needs and attitudes, to the important 'outer' concerns. Thus there is a focus on the desire for partnership and, ruled by Venus, on important loves. With the Taurus Sun here, there is a desire to be connected to someone in a close personal way, so marriage and relationships are important.

The Eighth House: House of Sex, Birth, Death and Reincarnation

I mean, no one asks beauty secrets of me, or 'What size do you wear?' or 'Who's your couturier?' They ask me about really deep things and I love that.
Shirley MacLaine

The eighth house is often described as the home of the 'life force'. Sex is here, also death, transformation and reincarnation and 'born again' religious experiences. Generally, what happens in the eighth house is deep and important. A Taurus with their Sun located here will be focused and intense and more likely to be secretive about their true desires.

The Ninth House: House of Philosophy and Travel

I'm not a beach bum. Although I prefer hot holidays, I always like to keep busy. As long as I can play sport on holiday, I'm happy.
Andy Murray

Travel and foreign languages, and also the various 'inner' journeys, spiritual or philosophical, that may be engaged in, are expressed through the 9th house. It also covers higher education, dreams and ideals. A Taurus with their Sun here will enjoy long distance travel and everything associated with other cultures including spiritual journeys.

The Tenth House: House of Social Identity and Career

Intelligence without ambition is a bird without wings.
Salvador Dali

The tenth house is steady and practical and is most easily and commonly abbreviated to being the 'career house'. It is about ambitions and worldly progress, and also covers authority in all its forms, how people react to it and how they deal with having authority over others. The tenth is generally seen as a pretty hard-headed and practical part of our chart. With the Taurus Sun here, an individual will be concerned with how others see them, as a desire for worldly success is embedded deep within.

The Eleventh House: House of Social Life and Friendships

The best place a person can die is where they die for others.
James M. Barrie

The eleventh house picks up where the tenth ends, but it covers non-material aspirations and ambitions, social conscience, social life and wider circles of friends. This house also governs altruism. Some modern astrologers would also put our attitude towards ecology here. A Taurus expresses this house in a practical way but still yearns for freedom and a connection to wider ideas.

The Twelfth House: House of Spirituality

He who is cruel to animals becomes hard also in his dealings with men. We can judge the heart of a man by his treatment of animals.
Immanuel Kant

The last house, the twelfth, has the potential to be our final state of learning and desire when we resolve all the developments of the other eleven houses. It can, however, also be the full accumulation of all the mistakes we have made in life, and is associated with secrecy, silence and escapism. With the Taurus Sun here, there is a need to escape the harsh realities of life, if only by soaking in the bath for hours and maybe, even, a tendency to shyness.

Chapter Six

The Difficulties

Now that you know a little about Taurus, what motivates one, how they 'view' their world and what interests them and makes them feel safe, we will now discuss what help they will need in a state of upsetment.

I see clients in private practice. They bring all sorts of what I call 'upsetments' to me to help sort out. They come for solutions, so I have to have quite a big box of solutions to offer them and (now) years of personal experience in that wonderful dance we call 'life'.

Most of my clients don't moan too much about their Taurus partners, but occasionally I will hear some grumblings and these are a few examples of them.

'My Taurus has filled the roof space, garage, spare bedroom and outhouse with "things we might need one day, just in case" and won't throw anything away.'

This is a common complaint about Taurus. Their inability to throw anything away.

It comes from a deep fear of poverty and lack, and needs a strong, firm constitution to correct.

What you must *never* do is gaily 'tidy up' their things or throw stuff away without consulting them. This will cause a mountain of sulks.

The best way to tackle the overcrowding situation is to draw a clean line of demarcation between what is yours and what is theirs and also where 'things' can be stored.

If you start off by making 'throwing things away' a fun activity, you shouldn't have too many problems. Devote one day a week or month to recycling or giving extra things away.

I had a Taurus boss once. He would make me keep old elastic bands that the postman/woman had left behind from his/her deliveries. I had to put them in a jar. I also had to keep all the packaging that the stock was delivered in. I worked in a designer jewellers and I, to this day, can't understand where his fear of loss came from. I drew the line at keeping old jars that he'd had his lunch soup in, or old yoghurt containers. He kept old screws and nails and all sorts of useless stuff and if he had to use something he'd 'saved' he rejoiced in his economy.

I wept at the time wasting.

I would have been far better off spending my time serving customers, or changing the displays than accumulating junk...

'My Taurus doesn't want to go out any more because he/she says it's too expensive and why don't we just stay at home?'

If your Taurus is very happy poodling along, doing their own thing, then the personal necessity to 'go out' and 'do 'stuff' will reduce.

Don't get all worked up!

All you have to do is explain, carefully, that you feel better going out and being sociable. Give them the choice to join you if they want to, but don't get all frazzled if they don't. If you're a social butterfly Gemini or an active Aries, sitting quietly at home won't appeal. It's not a problem to your Taurus, so don't make it one; just have separate social lives and, every now and then, do something or go somewhere together.

If it's a financial issue, then make sure you pay for your own activities.

I'm all for couples having separate bank accounts. I've never had a joint one and I don't want to start one now. I know so many people that fall out over money, I keep mine for my needs and my husband and I 'pay each other back' for joint expenses.

'My Taurus takes SO long to do anything...'

I generally hear this from parents of Taurus children. If you're a Fire sign, your Taurus child will seem to take forever just to get dressed in the morning.

You cannot hurry a Taurus.

I'll repeat that: YOU CANNOT HURRY A TAURUS.

So please don't try. It will only end in tears. If they take longer to 'do' something, you will have to plan ahead and start much earlier getting ready.

My Taurus husband gets up so early (I'm not marvellous first thing) as he likes to take his time doing things.

I get up in a flurry and rush around, at a fast pace, to catch up. I'm invariably late and generally rush out of the house with minutes to spare.

As my husband has started earlier than me (a bit like the hare and the tortoise story), he's always ready on time.

Again. Don't worry about this or make a fuss as it's wired into their consciousness to 'be prepared' and they will need far more time to get themselves washed, dressed and ready for the day. There is no right or wrong way, but hurrying a Taurus who is desperately trying to do things in a certain way will only flummox them and slow them down.

If you have to get up earlier to get your Taurus child ready for school, then set the alarm and reduce your levels of stress.

'My Taurus doesn't want to sell our house and move to somewhere bigger / smaller / nearer to work...'

When a Taurus buys a house and 'settles down', the last thing they want to do is sell up and move.

Argh! How could you do this? Make them get rid of something that they've grown to love, that contains all the things they like, in the places they like?

Again, you will need a lot of patience to make a Taurus feel good about selling up and moving house. They don't like doing it.

I've had clients who would rather get divorced than lose the house. Or if they do get divorced, their biggest grief will be the loss of their home and all the energy, memories and belongings associated with that home.

The only way to persuade a Taurus to move is if it's work-related. Plenty of Taureans will move house if their jobs demand it, because it's a salary/financial issue.

If you 'make your case' on a money-related basis, they will be with you all the way, but if you want to relocate just because of what they consider to be a whim, you will have a battle on your hands. And that battle will be a stubborn, relentless, obstinate and gruelling one.

* * *

As this is a helpful book, I'm now going to include some everyday types of issues that people have with their Taurus partners:

'My Taurus man finds it so hard to express his feelings about me. I tell him I love him and he says: "I have nothing but love for you." I finally just stopped saying anything that I feel for him because he doesn't like giving it back in return.'

This lady is obviously very demonstrative and, by the sound of it, is probably a Leo. She likes to hear, *often*, that she is loved. Once a week, or every now and then, or on her birthday won't be enough. In fact if she *is* a Leo, it would have to be at least 5 or 6 times a day!

Here we have a young Taurus man's reasoning. I love to hear other Sun signs' point of view and if we listen carefully we will hear their thinking processes:

'I am a Taurus man (age 20) and in my case I don't talk at all...I am

*really the silent type; when I am with a person I love I talk – a lot –
because I want her to feel safe / at home when she's with me... I am
an extremely affectionate person, so instead of telling her I love her,
I just hug her and hold her close and that's how I tell her how I feel
about her...*

*I am more of a body-language type of person. I communicate with
my body, hence I am short with words.*

*I'm not sure what kind of Taurus your boyfriend is, but if a girl
would tell me she loves me, and she means it, I'd do anything to let
her know that I love her more and that she is SAFE!*

*There was one time I kissed my girlfriend on New Year's Eve and
she cuddled up to me and whispered to me that she feels safe with me
– best night of my life.'*

As you can understand, he wants his lady to 'feel safe' because
that is what he wants to feel: safe and secure, so he ensures in a
practical way that his lady is just those things. And I thought it
was lovely how he remembered what she'd said on New Year's
Eve, that she felt safe with him.

This does work two ways; it's not just a Taurus man thing:

*'I'm a Virgo. My girlfriend (of three and a half months) is a Taurus
and I find things very difficult with her. She's a lovely, sweet and
gentle woman, and incredibly sexy with it. She doesn't talk about
our relationship so I have no idea where she thinks it's going, where
she might want it to go, if she thinks I'm just someone to have a bit
of fun with or a potential life partner. She has a very busy life, which
I just have to fit into and I just feel that she isn't all that bothered
about me. Meanwhile I feel that I'm falling for her, though I've had
to try to cool my emotions recently as it was starting to hurt that she
wasn't reciprocating. Being with her physically feels great, but she
is so uncommunicative that I have no idea if what I am doing is right
or if she's satisfied. It feels nice but I need verbal confirmation.'*

Remember what we said in earlier chapters about the body being important to a Taurus? You can talk all you like, but unless your bodies are in sync, no amount of conversation will alter things.

And why the *need* to talk? That's not something that this Earth sign focuses on. Notice their actions.

For a Taurus that means cooking, making them feel safe by providing a home with heating and food, comforts like comfy chairs and a comfortable bed, giving them a lift when it's raining, washing the clothes and ironing them nicely, watching favourite programmes on the television or listening to music they enjoy.

Taurus must be the only sign that can do what I call 'sit'. They can sit for hours, just looking out of the window. There is no urge to 'do'. Leave that to the Fire signs. No need to chat; leave that to the Air signs. No need to feel emotionally connected; leave that to the Water signs.

A Taurus just wants to 'be'.

Sort of Zen-like really.

Be safe.

Be secure.

Be.

Chapter Seven

The Solutions

Taurus psychotherapist Sigmund Freud defined happiness as, in the strictest sense, 'the (preferably sudden) satisfaction of needs which have been dammed up to a high degree'.

As the title of this book suggests, we're learning how to help a Taurus *feel* satisfied. Before we get any further into the solutions, I just want to define what satisfaction actually is:

Satisfy: fulfil expectations, or desires [of someone], be adequate, content, please.

Before you can fulfil someone's expectations, you need to ask what those expectations are. One thing that will drive a Taurus crazy is if you don't *ask* what it is that they like/want or need and just assume you know.

If you ask: 'How can I satisfy you?' 'How can I make you feel secure?' 'How can I meet your desires?' this will be music to their ears...

Then listen to those replies.

They won't repeat them; they will probably only tell you once and you will only have to ask them once for yours to be fulfilled.

Here's the Taurus author of *To Kill a Mockingbird*, Harper Lee, talking about repeating herself: *'I have said what I wanted to say and I will not say it again.'*

A Taurus won't want to have an Air sign discussion about the whys and wherefores of those choices. They might tell you that they love steak. Or cabbages. Or soft satin. They will answer the questions and expect an action...

I asked a few Taureans what made them feel satisfied.

Yankel is studying at a UK university. Here she tells me how she feels when she's satisfied:

The Solutions

'I feel satisfied only when things I'm doing are perfect, no matter what it is: excellent final paper or just a good meal.'

Nina tells us:

'...helping others, achievement.'

Celia feels satisfied in a number of ways:

'My life! Now, and when I look back over it! More specifically, when I get a bit of gardening and a bit of writing done as part of my day, and some bhakti yoga (devotional chanting).'

Caroline (who is also an author) tells us:

'Writing, finishing a good book. Being spiritual. Eating down-to-earth food.'

I loved the way she said 'down-to-earth food' – that was such a Taurus statement. No nouvelle cuisine for her then!

Marla tells us some of her satisfaction-prompts:

'A good meal. Having everything done that needed to be done at the end of the day. (Completing lists.) Having a good workout and the fresh feeling I get afterwards. Washing my hair and having a shower at the end of a strenuous day gardening, and being able to look at what I have done that day. Completing sewing job/jobs, making myself something I can wear.'

Famous musician and Taurus Yehudi Menuhin tells us about his work and how, when conducting, all he has to do is make a little gesture and the orchestra responds:

'They are sensitive; they know me well and I know them. I can, with

59

some little gesture, evoke something which they recognize as an intention which hasn't ever been before. It's a lovely sensation; it gives one really the sensation of riding a stallion – something that responds. It understands the situation. It's a wonderful satisfaction.'

One thing is for sure. If you want your Taurus to feel satisfied, they need to have somewhere they can call 'home'. Now, this is different from what a Cancer calls home. They don't care where the home is, as long as it exists and has a main carer on duty; it could be in a hut in a desert – it wouldn't matter. But when it comes to a 'home' for a Taurus, it needs to be slightly different from that. It needs to be a home-base, as it will affect them for the rest of their lives.

My lovely husband's parents lived in the same house for all of his life. Then when his father died, his mother refused to move and carried on living there until her death.

One of the most difficult things for my husband to get through was the selling of the family home. It wasn't that he even lived there any more. It wasn't that he *wanted* to live there any more, but when he saw, on the estate agent's website, pictures of his childhood home, with a picture of the chair his mother used to sit in, the Aga and the table in the dining room, it then brought into his consciousness that not only had his dear mother died, but also the place that held so many memories for him was going to be bought by someone else, lived in by someone else, not be 'his' any more.

He not only had to say goodbye to his mother but also to *his* whole earlier lifetime. As if part of his life died as well.

Now, your average Gemini or Aquarius or Aries would hardly bother about these things in this way. They don't equate any physical 'being' with their existence, but a Taurus does.

Celia is a Taurus, an author, mother, wife, grandmother, gardener and spiritual buddy for her Native American friends.

She spent her late thirties in Canada with the Arrow Lakes people and wrote about her experiences of living with them in her book *A Twist in Coyote's Tale*.

Here she describes moving with her 3 children into a new home. The building was previously used as a restaurant but was now being let out as a holiday home.

Moving a family into the ex-restaurant required some creative thinking. A skilled carpenter and joiner, within a couple of weeks the new owner had transformed the large restaurant into a bedroom and play room, while I reinvented the bar as a kitchen and the original dining room, a large, light, airy space punctuated by massive supporting logs the size of the telegraph poles, as a spacious open-plan living-area. One corner I screened off with plants and stained-glass; overlooking a fabulous view of the river, this was my sleeping-area. An elevated platform (its original function impossible to fathom) served as a loft-bedroom, while the split-level undercroft, with its own entrance and view over the river, made a perfect teenage hang-out.

This account is not your 'average' Taurus abode, but does describe wonderfully a Taurean's need to have a home, as without one they don't have a 'base camp' to operate from.

I know Taurus people who, when they're preparing to marry, will spend more time and energy getting the home organised, than preparing the actual ceremony itself. I also know more Taureans than I care to mention who will find it hard to leave a marriage because that house, that they've spent so many years funding, paying a mortgage for, repairing, painting, decorating, tending, cleaning, living in, damp-proofing, lagging, insulating, heating, carpeting, eating in, entertaining in, has become almost a part of themselves.

Remember: Taurus is practical and needs firm, grounded

practical solutions to most everyday problems.

You can modify slightly the help you give them by taking into account their Asc or Moon. Celia has a Gemini Ascendant, so she moved house a lot, but because she's a Taurus, *having* a house/home is high on her list of priorities.

The Bach Flower Essences will help too to settle any emotional upsetments.

Aries Asc or Moon

There is only one way to help this combo and that is to do something physical and/or sporty. Get on your running shoes or sports kit and meet up with your Taurus/Aries, and get them to thrash their feelings out on the tennis court, basketball court, football pitch, or anywhere that moves the body. If you want them to feel better, don't bother with conversation – ACTION is the needed solution. Try and avoid anything that might put you at risk, so don't arrange a fencing session or boxing match; you might find you're the target for any stressful feelings!

Taurus Asc or Moon

The energies for double Taurus are aimed at wanting to feel safe and secure. Arrange a firm date and take your double Taurus to a good slap-up meal, or at the very least cook for them. Slow down and match their body language. Get the chocolates and good wine out and ensure they're feeling relaxed. If you're any good at massage, you will be seen as their saviour, or hire someone qualified to smooth away those angsty energies with fragrant oils and soothing movements. The body needs to be attended to, so deep breathing and tactile contact is needed. The mind and other worries can be sorted out later.

Gemini Asc or Moon

Now you will have to have your wits about you and your ears peeled back. Pay attention to every word they say. A

Taurus/Gemini needs to feel heard and understood. If you repeat back a summary of what they've told you, you're on solid ground. Maybe even get them to write down how they feel, as they'll be so speeding around with questions and remarks and jibes and damning one-liners, you might get singed in the process. When they've written as much as they can, change the subject and do something totally different like going for a walk or meeting up with some other friends.

Cancer Asc or Moon

A Taurus/Cancer will want to feel their emotions. They will be overcome with them. In fact this might make them a little weepy. Get the tissues out and mirror their body language and, when they've cried their ocean, wrap them up in some soft, fluffy blanket and tuck them up on the sofa. Listen carefully to their words and look underneath what they're actually saying. Tune into their feelings, which at this moment will be like a wave, overwhelming and wet. In a little while, the wave will recede and they'll be back to normal. Hugs! Did I mention hugs? They will be needed in abundance when Taurus/Cancer gets down, so snuggle up and embrace the hurt away.

Leo Asc or Moon

Do NOT ignore a Taurus/Leo. They want to feel acknowledged and included. They will be running around, sighing and being dramatic and shouting 'Off with their heads!' or similar drastic cries. Ignore the drama but don't ignore the person. You could ask, 'What will help you *now*?' and do whatever they suggest, provided it's legal and do-able. Agree that life is unfair and lay out the red carpet of one-to-one special treatment with personal inclusion. Say their name more than once, in friendly tones. This always works a treat, and nod your head in agreement to their feelings, which by now will be buzzing around at an alarming rate. Get them to take one good, deep breath in...and slowly let it out…and their sunny self will soon return.

Virgo Asc or Moon

With the Taurus/Virgo person you will need to ooze calm and be centred. Remember the Flower Essence Centaury and administer 2 drops in water before you attempt any other form of help. What is needed is for their brains to switch off. They have active, fast-moving brains; couple that with Virgo's need for precision and all they can think about is how to 'make things better' and they will be striving to 'do' millions of things about it all. The worst-case scenario will see them like rabbits in the headlamps, frozen on one recurring idea, which they find hard to break out of. Soothing music, Tai Chi, gentle body exercise, sensible food, lots of good sleep will bring them back to earth perfectly.

Libra Asc or Moon

Most Taurus/Libra combos will be worried about relation-ships…or 'The One'. If they've fallen out with their nearest and dearest you will find a weepy, questioning person needing careful handling. First off, don't give them any choices. This is, after all, the person who will be deliberating a choice. Come or go? Stay or leave? Right or wrong? Help the process by *not* giving a choice, and sweep them away to somewhere beautiful and presentable where they can experience a better balance of ideas. Don't correct them or get into an argument. Don't talk too much, let the place you have chosen calm them enough to reconfigure, and let them feel centred. Yoga, gentle massage, light, tuneful music – harp or something equally soothing – will work well too.

Scorpio Asc or Moon

Stand back! Don't get too close when Taurus/Scorpio lets rip. You will find them consumed with the passion of deep, excruciating, painful feelings, and revenge might be on the agenda. Be aware that they will want to resolve whatever is going on with drastic, painful solutions. If you think about the colour of deep red blood you will get an idea of how they're feeling. It sucks! It's horrible! They want an END to it all (whatever is happening to them).

Get them to write the person or problem a letter. Tell them to put ALL their feelings into the writing...then make a bonfire or light a candle and safely watch the pain and anguish be consumed by the flames. Be firm. Be 'there'. You can't do much other than wait out the feelings, which, like all feelings, will eventually subside.

Sagittarius Asc or Moon

To get a Taurus/Sag to admit that there is a problem will be difficult. It's generally 'them' that are the problem, so 'they' will have to be the focus of the solution. Get some aged texts. The Bible, or other friendly spiritual writings by a favourite guru or lama or other spiritual leader, and either lend or buy the book for them. Arrange a trip away to some far-off exotic land where they can 'escape' from the everyday-ness that has caused the problem. If finances are tight, get them to a local foreign restaurant or talk where the focus is on far-off and distant lands. McDonald's or take-aways won't work the same. They need to be surrounded by people and conversations that are different from their own, so they can feel free to have the thoughts/feelings and opinions they're having. If they enjoy sport, go to a game – anything that will be different from where they are at the moment. Change, exotic change, is paramount.

Capricorn Asc or Moon

As Capricorn is ruled by Saturn and loves serious, sensible solutions, a Taurus/Cappie will want the advice and guidance from someone older and hopefully wiser than them. Their main worry will be about 'the future' and they will be concerned that they've ruined their chances, or missed an opportunity. If you can find someone who has 'been there and done that', they will start to thaw a little. You could of course go one better and help them discover their ancestral line and help them research their family tree as Taurus/Cap loves that which is ancient and tried and tested. A short visit to a stately home or traditional concert might also help...and do NOT rush them to recover. They need time and space.

Aquarius Asc or Moon

If you can imagine the weirdest and wackiest solution to their problem, you will have found the elixir of happiness. Taurus/Aqua loves that which can only be defined as 'unusual'. Stay away from mainstream ideas; go for that which is different and unregulated and you'll have the happiest Taurus/Aqua on the planet. Staying up late discussing Life, the Universe and Everything will also go down well. You could take them out for a short trip to see street entertainers, or meet with some art students or people co-creating an ecological event. You could plug them into a simulator so they can experience some wacky occurrence, or play a computer game that doesn't have any set rules. Anything that is not normal, not regular, not Earth-based. They want to feel connected to some life-changing human consciousness.

Pisces Asc or Moon

Get out your Angel cards; light the incense or some candles. Put on soft music, get away from 'life' and 'humans', and touch into the outer reaches of all that is cosmic and divine. Any form of divination will be welcomed. They will be worrying about their next life, and their karma, so reassure them you've got that covered. The spiritual solution must be credible and not *too* fantastic or you'll lose them. They're still a practical Taurus underneath all the Pisces confusion. Keep their feet on the ground, but let their mind go where nothing hurts and no one can intervene. Meditation, hypnotherapy, relaxation, angels, fairies, stone circles or making a pilgrimage... All this will be welcome and, at the very least, a long, fragrant bath with a big 'Do Not Disturb' sign on the door!

Chapter Eight

Satisfying Tactics

Hopefully by now you will have made the birth chart for your Taurus nearest and dearest and determined what sign their Ascendant and Moon are.

You're armed with a Flower Essence or two and you feel better about knowing this person.

I will now give some tips about how you can experience Taurus energy in their different incarnations. A Taurus baby is definitely a different scenario from a Taurus boss. Those important qualities of being steady and steadfast will still be there, but you'll need to modify them slightly in each manifestation.

Your Taurus Child

What a distressing contrast there is between the radiant intelligence of the child and the feeble mentality of the average adult.
Sigmund Freud

I have never parented a Taurus child, and I hardly know any parents with Taurus children. I know a lot of Taureans but I didn't know them when they were small, so this advice has to come from the Taureans themselves. I can't imagine it too well myself.

I know all the traditional Taurus happiness-making things, but do they work well when they're growing up? I came to the conclusion that the child part of Taurus isn't that different from the adult version; it's just a little slower and steadier.

Marla, the flower therapist we met earlier, has a Leo Ascendant, so praise is very important to her. Here she talks about her childhood:

'As a child, I was very insecure. I was not heard or listened to much. My parents were worried I wasn't doing well enough in school when I was a young teenager. When they went to the open evening, they found I was about 3rd in my year. When they came home they told me I was doing 'OK' and I wasn't praised for my achievements. Consequently as a late teen I went off the rails a bit and became outrageous in dress and hairstyles, hoping to shock, especially my father. It worked. At least I got negative attention then! Looking back, if I had been nurtured, praised, encouraged and openly loved by both my parents (I don't remember my mum ever telling me she loved me, and my father definitely never said he loved me and couldn't express emotion, which now I understand came from his childhood), I wouldn't have had such a rocky start and got married too young to the wrong man just to leave home!'

I then asked my Taurus husband what things were important to him as a child and here are a few things he came up with:

'Needing a comfy bed, own space, meals on time, good food, routine, tactile contact, hugs and kisses, creativity – making model aeroplanes etc., being artistic, not too many questions, logical not complicated, beautiful scenery, walking/cycling, good music of a genre I liked, sense of ownership / owning things. Taureans don't like change as it disrupts the routine. Like to plan, ensuring the unexpected is not a threat and challenge to their own comfort zone. Feel safest in their comfort zone, don't like to be threatened, don't like to be criticised; being under threat is very uncomfortable. Like to be in control of immediate surroundings. If interrupted, or space is invaded, that's very stressful. Need a bedtime routine, a story, strokes to the head – they find that very relaxing.'

Routine makes a Taurus feel comfortable and satisfied. Changing things, or doing things differently, too often sends them into a spin. Don't do it!

Taurus Arthur Conan Doyle, writer of the Sherlock Holmes series of books, said: *'I have frequently gained my first real insight into the character of parents by studying their children.'*

I asked author Celia: What would you need to know to make you feel secure and loved as a child?

She replied:

'That it was perfectly acceptable not to want to be with other people and rather be alone, doing my own thing out in nature. That they missed me when I wasn't there.'

What would that parent need to do?

'Tell a child about stuff going on in the family, rather than "protecting" her; cuddle her often; tell/read her magical stories; listen to her stories.'

Mandy has Moon in Aquarius and is a retired homeopath. She told me what she would have liked her parents to understand, as she was growing up:

'I would need parents I could rely on (which I had) for housing and food and to know they were in control of what was happening. That was as a young child. From age 11 would have liked them to have been more fun and to have introduced me to more creative things like art. My dad just thought it was important to get a "good academic education", which didn't stimulate me at all. As an only child I was left to find my own stimulation, which I could do to a certain extent, but I would have liked to have been shown it was possible to be more adventurous and that those things were available. Would have liked my dad to realise the world went beyond maths, which I hated and was no good at, but he lived and breathed numbers and mathe-

matical problems.'

Marla gives us some insights to this question as not only is she a Taurus herself, but her oldest son is one too:

'As a mother of a Taurus, I have had to pull my son into line hard in the past and still do from time to time. I listen to him and share in a way I would never have been able to with my parents. As a result, I feel he is a balanced, caring, well-rounded man who is maturing well.'

Astrologer Anne also has good advice for parenting a Taurus:

'Taurean children need affection and gentle handling. Please don't tell them they're stubborn – they usually have a good reason for their behaviour, and if they're digging their heels in it's because they're afraid of something. Change is difficult, especially if it involves the possibility of losing a possession or a loved one. Addressing this fear will add to their sense of security and help them deal with the change. Sharing can be difficult and telling them they're selfish is counter-productive. The best thing to do is to gently appeal to their nurturing instinct – this usually does the trick. Finally, I would have loved the opportunity to have had a pet or spent time in nature. This only happened when I became an adult and I feel I missed out!'

Your Taurus Boss

As I mentioned earlier, I once had a Taurus boss. He was very happy to employ me, bought me flowers once when I hit a target, left me in charge of his valuable designer jewellery shop, but all that ended one sad and sorry day.

He didn't like people that smoked.

And while I was working there, I got into an emotional tangle with a boyfriend and started smoking again...outside the shop.

He was not impressed. I only did it once. But a little while later, I went into work and he wanted to see me in his office upstairs. I climbed the stairs, wondering what he wanted to talk to me about. Had I ordered the right stock? Had I hit my targets? Had I cleaned the shop to his liking? I couldn't work out why he wanted to see me when we normally spoke on the shop floor in the morning.

I got into the office and in less than 5 minutes I was walking out again, tears in my eyes, distraught as he'd just sacked me. He didn't say why either, but I know it was because of the smoking. I'd seriously let him down and done the very thing he'd so hated in other retailers: the sight of the staff standing outside the shop, puffing on a cigarette.

I asked his secretary if she knew what had happened, and all she would say to me was: I was one of many that had been 'let go'.

If you have a Taurus boss, male or female, make sure you *establish right at the beginning* exactly what they will agree to and what they won't. This will be an unchanging reality. If they tell you they like fresh flowers on a Monday, remember that. If they say they like their martini shaken not stirred, again pay attention. If they tell you they don't like smoking, nothing you say will change their mind or their opinion.

Nothing.

I learned the hard way but actually in reality he did me a favour, because then I had to concentrate my energies on my career as a homeopath and later as an astrologer, and I would not have been able to do that if I was still selling earrings and necklaces.

Taurus and Love

Doubt thou the stars are fire;
Doubt that the sun doth move;
Doubt truth to be a liar;
But never doubt I love.
Shakespeare (from *Hamlet*)

Without doubt, all signs of the Zodiac love to love and be loved, but Taurus (and Libra) is ruled by the Goddess of Love: Venus, and therefore has a deeper access to the truth of love.

If your astrological ruler is all about love, then you're more likely to be tuned into the subject. The difference between Libra love and Taurus love is that Taurus is more earthy, more grounded and certainly more practical.

So, few Taureans will endure a long-distance romance or one that is complicated or complex.

I have a female relative who didn't fall in love and marry until she was in her fifties and now she is the happiest woman as her husband shares the same interests (they met in church). She wasn't prepared to take second best and held out until 'Mr Right' made an appearance. That Taurus patience stood her in good stead.

Your (Female) Taurus Lover

To successfully date your (female) Taurus lover you will have to throw away any ideas of rushing her or pushing her to do something she doesn't want to do.

Here we have Diana, on a dating site, telling us what she's looking for in a relationship and a little bit about herself. If you ever want to learn what motivates a Sun sign, I suggest you visit a dating site and see how the descriptions people write about themselves match exactly their Sun signs...even if they have no interest in Astrology.

About Me:

'After listening to my boss give (unsolicited) advice on "how to get a fella" (most of which annoyed the feminist in me) I decided it was time to look for my Mr Darcy. (From Bridget Jones's Diary, not Pride and Prejudice.)

'All my attempts at pretending to be a thinner Nigella Lawson have been met with disaster – I've been known to burn an egg. I went to a cricket match last year, and was asking how many goals had been scored. And apparently, these are the talents I need to "get a fella". (I was listening while pretending I couldn't roll my eyes back far enough.)

'What I am though, according to my brother, is laid-back and sweet. I also like to flip my hair while making witty remarks. Despite working in the city I am a happy person; it takes a lot to faze me. I am a feminist (hadn't you noticed?) and refuse to let a man buy me dinner. We'll go Dutch instead. I used to be one of those people who throw paint on celebrities wearing fur, but sadly, I'm reformed now.

'Oh and I have nice eyes.'

Who I'm Looking For:

'A good cuddler. And someone who is organised enough to actually book and do things, instead of just reading about them on Timeout like I do.'

So, there you are, hoping to date a Taurus woman. Here are a few ideas of what you will need to know.

First of all you will need to make a firm date. A time and a place and stick to it. Don't make a vague attempt at a meeting, or your Taurus woman will be confused and upset.

Don't expect her to suggest where to meet either. That's your job.

Make sure you're early, as she will be. She might not be sitting in the chair at the bar as arranged, but she will have parked her car, or be in the ladies adjusting her hair/make-up/clothes and checking she looks presentable.

Make sure, on the first date, that you either touch her hand gently, or accidently stroke her arm, or softly touch her body in some (sensible) way by helping her off with her coat. If you want to impress her, open the door for her, or pull her chair out for her. If you do anything 'old fashioned' or 'retro' she will be in your life forever.

Don't make your first date too complicated. She's not a Sagittarius and won't want to go on a cycling 'adventure'. She's not an Aries, so she won't want to go somewhere busy or exciting. She's not a Leo, so she won't want to go to the theatre; and she's not a Gemini, so don't suggest the cinema.

Your options will include one of the following:

A meal, a drink, a slow walk in a nature reserve / National Trust property / garden / by the seaside, quiet chat in a secluded location, visit to an art gallery, comfy home-cooked meal or a drink, short drive to somewhere romantic/beautiful.

Your first date doesn't have to be an all-swinging, all-dancing complete entertainment.

Your (Male) Taurus Lover

Dating a Taurus man is slightly different from dating a Taurus woman. All those key pointers of taking time, not rushing and being tactile are needed though.

Nadine is a white witch and alternative therapist. She lives and works in the West Country near me and we're both Pisces and both ended up with Taurus as our second husbands! Here she tells us about her experiences of dating a Taurus man:

'Having a Taurean boyfriend and then husband was very different for me, my first husband being a hot-headed Leo. When we were going out I absolutely had to wait for him to make the plans – which

was excruciating! Dates were always lovely though, with arrangements being perfect, doors being opened and excellent food – Taureans know what they like!

'Trustworthy, dependable and solid are words I would use to describe my hubby – but with a wicked sense of humour! If you want an opinion it will be fair and balanced and not always popular, but based on sound knowledge and good intuition.

'On the down side, never expect a quick decision – buying a car takes months of research! Also never borrow his stuff or try to share his food if you don't want raised eyebrows and indignation!'

That sounds like good advice. Let's see what's happening on the dating websites.

Here we have Jacob, a 28-year-old nature conservation officer, looking for love.

About Me:

'Thanks for stopping by.

'It's quite relaxing here…one easy-going bloke who still doesn't quite know what he wants but every day gets a little more comfortable with that idea! Less work and more spare time is the current plan. I like to do stuff; for instance in the last week I've been to Snowdon, bought a rug, joined a mindfulness course, gone to a 4-day week.

'That was a pretty busy week though. By the way, that profile picture looks nothing like me. Must have been good lighting or something. I literally have no idea who that is. The only thing I've got in common with that picture is that I don't show my teeth when smiling. Strangely I have quite nice teeth.'

Who I'm Looking For:

'Would you come for a country or London walk?
'Laugh at yourself if you get cream on your nose?

'Are you hopefully romantic, believing that in a world full of break-ups, happy singletons and divorcees, you'll make a good choice and do it right?

'You need to be comfortable with the surname of Ringhouse, as if we get married that's what you're going to get. Yes, it's horrendous; you always run out of room on those forms that have the computer-read boxes where you write your name. But hey ho, it could be Higginbottom or Pratt. Thinking about it, it's probably best to keep your own name.'

As mentioned above about the female Taurus lover, you will have to accept that your first date is not going to be white-water rafting on the Arkansas River, Colorado; leave that to the Sagittarians. It also won't be hosting a drama workshop in Glastonbury; leave that to the Leos.

Nope! Your first date, as Jacob says, will involve a walk, preferably in the country (as he works in nature conservation).

'Crikey,' you might think. 'That sounds a little boring!'

But slow down, Miss Rushy!

Taking a nice leisurely walk in the country can be very entertaining. He might know the names of all the bird songs, and point them out to you as you walk. He might ask you all about yourself and listen *really* carefully. He might even have planned that your walk will culminate in a rustic pub with a romantic log-fire to keep away the cold. And when you get there, he might already know what food you like and what drink you prefer, because he will have asked those questions while you walked...

Doesn't that sound better? Being listened to and appreciated? Who needs white-water rafting now?

What to Do If Your Taurus Relationship Ends

Fire sign

If you are a Fire sign – Aries, Leo or Sagittarius – you will need something active and exciting to help you get over your relationship ending.

You will also need to use the element of Fire in your healing process.

Get a nice night-light candle and light it and recite: 'I... (your name) do let you... (your Taurus's name) go, in freedom and with love, so that I am free to attract my true soul-love.'

Leave the night light in a safe place to completely burn away. Allow at least an hour. In the meantime gather up any belongings or possessions that are your now ex-lover's and deliver them back to your Taurus. It's polite to telephone first and notify your ex when you will be arriving.

If you have any photos of you together or other mementos or even gifts, don't be in a rush to destroy them, as some Fire signs are prone to do. Better to put them away in a box in the attic or garage until you feel a little less upset.

In a few months' time, go through the box and keep the things you like and give away the things you don't.

Earth sign

If you are an Earth sign – Taurus, Virgo or Capricorn – you will feel less inclined to do something dramatic or outrageous. It might also take you slightly longer to recover your equilibrium, so allow yourself a few weeks and a maximum of three months to grieve.

You will be using the Earth element to help your healing. with the use of some trusty crystals.

The best crystals to use are the ones associated with your Sun sign and also with protection.

Taurus = Emerald

Virgo = Agate

Capricorn = Onyx

Cleanse your crystal in fresh running water. Wrap it in some pretty silk fabric, then go on a walk into the countryside. When you find a suitable spot that is quiet and where you won't be disturbed, dig a small hole and place your crystal in the ground.

Spend a few minutes thinking about your relationship, the good times and the bad. Forgive yourself for any mistakes you may have made.

Imagine a beautiful plant growing from the ground where you have buried your crystal, and the plant blossoming and growing strong.

This will represent your new love that will be with you when the time is right.

Air sign

If you're an Air sign – Gemini, Libra or Aquarius – you might want to talk about what happened first before you finish the relationship. Air signs need reasons and answers, and can waste precious life-energy looking for those answers. You might need to meet with your Taurus to tell him/her exactly what you think/thought about his/her opinions, ideas and thoughts. You might also be tempted to tell him/her what you think about them now, which I do not recommend.

Far better to put those thoughts into a tangible form by writing your ex-Taurus a letter. It is not a letter that you are actually going to post, but you are going to put as much energy into it as if you were actually going to send it.

Write to them thus: 'Dear Mr/Ms/Miss Taurus, I expect you will be happy now in your new life, but there are a few things I would like to know and understand before I say goodbye.'

Then list all the annoying, aggravating and upsetting things your (now ex) Taurus indulged in. Make a list as long as you like. Put in as much detail as you feel comfortable with, including things like how many times they worried about the bills, or wouldn't let you throw anything away, or stayed indoors all year.

Keep writing till you can write no more, then end your letter with something like: 'Even though we were not suited, and I suffered because of this, I wish you well on your path.' Or some other positive comment.

Then tear your letter into teeny little pieces and put them into a small container. We are now going to use the element of Air to rectify the situation.

Take a trip to somewhere windy and high, like the top of a hill, and when you're ready, open your container and sprinkle a few random pieces of your letter into the wind. Don't use the entire letter or you run the risk of littering, just enough pieces to be significant.

Watch those little pieces of paper fly into the distance and imagine them connecting with the nature spirits.

Your relationship has now ended.

Water sign

If you are a Water sign – Cancer, Scorpio or Pisces – you might find it more difficult to recover quickly from your relationship. You might find yourself weeping at inopportune moments, or when you hear your song on the radio, or when you see other couples happily being in each other's company. You might lie awake at night worrying that you have ruined your life, and your ex-Taurus is having all the fun. As you might have gathered by now, this is unlikely. Your ex might be as upset as you.

Your emotional healing therefore needs to incorporate the Water element.

As you are capable of weeping for England, the next time you are in floods of tears capture one small teardrop and place it into a small glass. Have one handy just for this purpose. Decorate it if you feel like it. Small flowers, stars, or twinkly things.

Now fill your glass to the top with tap water and place it on a table.

Then recite the following:

'This loving relationship with you ... (your ex-Taurus' name)
    has ended.
I reach out across time and space to you.
My tears will wash away the hurt I feel.
I release you from my heart, mind and soul.
We part in peace.'

And then slowly drink the water. Imagine your hurt dissolving away, freeing you from all anxieties and releasing you from sadness.

Then spend the next few weeks being nice to yourself. If you need to talk, find someone you trust, and confide in them. Keep tissues handy.

Your Taurus Friend

I have a few very dear Taurus friends. They're loyal, fun to be with, have a cracking sense of humour, are great cooks or at least know where to eat good food, and have the capacity to always help me understand other people's points of view.

While I was training to be a homeopath my Taurus supervisor and I became very close and that friendship withstood eight years working together as volunteers in a charity for the homeless and/or people with addictions. She would always turn up to work on time, with her thermos flask and sandwiches, as she'd rather have her lunch unhurried when she arrived. Unlike me, who would wolf down some food, then race across town on my motor-scooter.

She would be the gentle 'observer' and I would be the 'inquisitor'. If the client was very disturbed mentally and she couldn't keep up with the conversation, I'd chip in and take over, giving the client feedback and prompts. We became a dynamic team and I enjoyed every minute of that work.

When she decided she wanted to stop working there, that was it. There was nothing I could say to change her mind. Remember my Taurus boss? Once the Bull has made up their mind, forget trying to change it. It's a waste of energy.

If I want a practical solution to a problem, I will turn to my Taurus friends. Each one of them has that practical, sensible world organised and can impart their knowledge to me in words of not more than two syllables so I can understand and use the information. If you want to understand something that you're finding difficult, ask a Taurus to explain it to you. In fact, if you want to learn even more, get a Taurus to *show* you, as they're generally very good with their hands.

If you're a Fire or Air sign, I don't recommend you spend too much time with your Taurus friend as you might exhaust each other. Taurus can't travel at such mental or physical speeds as yourself, and can easily get lost in conversations that are too quick.

If they have Mercury in Taurus too, their ability to snap back with witty replies will be far less. They need time to think and work out strategies.

Your Taurus Mother

If your mother is a Taurus it will either help or hinder you, depending on what sign you are. If you're a Fire or Air sign, your body and surroundings might be all sorted, but your energy and mind are frazzling into non-existence.

Don't let this become a problem. If your parent is a different element from you, there are plenty of remedies and tips to help.

Laima is a multi-lingual creative writing student and a Gemini and lives in Lithuania. She tells us what it's like for her to have an Earth sign Taurus mother:

'Having a Taurus mother means being fed, clothed and having a tidy environment. My mother always thought in advance that I don't have a sweater for the upcoming cold season, or I need a new coat, or a scarf...Even if for me the season seems still far away and I don't

even get any thoughts of it happening. Since I still lived with my parents during my first studies, that practical physical care was very noticeable during the exams. I'd sit in my room studying for hours and my mother would come and ask what would I like to eat and then come with food, always making sure my main body needs are taken care of. She's also obsessed with everything being tidy and always used to (and still does) complain that seeing my room will give her a heart attack one day (as I have stuff everywhere, all over the place, but that's the only way I can find everything!).

'But on the negative side, she never asked how I felt, or anything much outside the practical stuff. I felt like I am being constantly monitored; she had to know where I am and what I'm doing every minute of the day. I would barely set my foot into the house and the phone is already ringing to check if I'm home. But she never knew me as a person and never tried to. She never encouraged my plans or dreams; whenever I tried voicing one she would end up saying something like "We'll see how it turns out", or "But that requires this and that". I'm not stupid; I know what it requires – I don't need someone else pointing it out. I need someone to tell me, "Go, try, good luck!" Even my choices of what to study were discussed not in terms of what I like or what I want, but what job can I take after graduating and how well will it pay. Practical "objective" aspects of everything were always considered more important than my own feelings.

'After all this complaining I should say that in the last few years she's improved greatly and really is trying to see my side of things and what's important to me :) Otherwise I wouldn't be in London, studying creative writing. But in general that's the case: she was great at taking care of the practical stuff, but not listening to what I have to say or how I feel. Whenever I expressed an idea, she had to bring me down with scepticism or pointing out a list of requirements (as if it's not obvious as it is), when all I needed was believing in me.

'And something I've been saying for a while. She thought I am

immature because I don't pay enough attention to the practical material stuff. I thought she hasn't "evolved" and gained any wisdom because she ONLY cares about the primitive material stuff.

'Oh, and one more thing: it's impossible to win an argument with a Taurus. Even if you point it out that they're wrong, they will start saying things like "I don't want to talk to you any more", "That's it, let's stop this right now!", "I'll talk to you when you calm down" or anything else, just to avoid facing the fact that they're wrong.

'My Leo friend also has a Taurus mother. He told me once: "If a Taurus needs the fridge to be blue, in order to win an argument, then it's blue, and you can do whatever you want to try and point out that it's obviously white. If they need it to be blue, then it's blue – nothing you can do about it."

'Frustrating as hell. You can never have an intelligent argument with them.'

Yes, this is true.

Your average Taurus won't want to 'have an argument' as, to their way of thinking, that's a complete waste of precious time, which could be spent much more productively. Air and Fire signs love to jabber and argue and 'discuss', as my Libra son calls it, but us Water signs (and the Earth signs) are no good at verbal ping-pong and prefer to talk to express feelings, not talk about 'ideas'.

However, if you're a Water or Earth sign, your Taurus mother will be a Goddess. You will be clothed, fed, dressed appropriately for the current weather conditions in clean clothes. You will have routine, which all children enjoy. You will have someone there in the background encouraging you from start to finish. Celebrating, in their own quiet way, your achievements.

Taurus author Jodi Picoult enjoys being a Mom. Here she talks about her teenager daughter:

'Even teenagers love to snuggle! Having that moment of connection with your children – there's nothing like that. Last night, my daughter, who is 16, patted her bed and said, "Come sit down, Mom." And I said, "What do you want me to do? Tuck you in? Give you a kiss goodnight?" And she said, "No, come here." Then she lifted the covers so I could get in and snuggle with her. And for a 16-year-old, that was great. We just kind of sat there and talked for a little while. I'll never forget it. Next time, it'll be my idea!'

However, if your Taurus mother gets stressed, her ability to be an Earth Goddess will be more difficult.

Taurus singer Cher is mother to her Sun Pisces, Moon Virgo daughter Chastity. Their relationship took a turn for the worse when Chastity decided to become Chaz and have a sex change. Cher took it badly at first but eventually came round to his new life. Chaz explained:

'For parents this could be something that's kind of hard to deal with. It's a process of grieving for a child you've lost and adjusting to the new one taking their place. It takes a lot of time. She sticks up for me – and what an ally to have. We are developing a new relationship.'

All Taureans hate change and the changes Cher had to make were profound, but over the years she has accepted this change.

'The day that we talked about it, really talked about it seriously, I said, "If you have to do this you just have to do it." I wasn't always able to be quite as calm through the process, but that day I was so calm, and just thought, "This is what has to happen."'

If your mother is Taurus, remember that the physical world and the world of beauty are incredibly important to her. I've lost track of the amount of Taurus mothers I know who also paint or create in some way. They tend to put these creative pursuits to one side while they are raising a family but I think that actually makes them less happy. If they can combine being creative and being a mother, they are fulfilling more of their life path.

Your Taurus Father

Your Taurus father will be 'Mr Practical'.

If you want something repaired or put together, or mended, your Taurus father will be champion. Taurus men love to have something to solve and organise, so they are happiest making sense of the complicated world we live in. Don't expect your Taurus father to be terribly keen on anything too digital or computer-based as, unless they can physically experience something, they find it harder to value.

But things like new tyres for the car, or a heater for the living room, or a good lick of paint in the bedroom will keep your Taurus dad busy.

Here we have Lewis debating about his finances before he becomes a father. He wants to be able to *'financially look after this child until it can look after itself'*.

This is something he easily gets to grips with.

Assessing My Financial Situation:

'I am about as middle class as you can get, probably even in the lower part of that. The little perks in my life consist of the scattered trip (once a year), a few extra channels (gotta have my HBO), a decent car, pets, a house (that the bank owns), one night out a week, playing sports, and the odd personal purchase under $30. Needless to say, with that lifestyle, I almost live paycheck to paycheck. I am not in a lot of debt, but I don't have as much breathing room as I would like.

'Now, I am really starting to think about my finances. I've already taken a look at my lifestyle and I am making changes there. Now, the fact remains that I will need to financially look after this

baby for his/her life, or until my child can look after itself. And by the example set by some of my friends, some still living at home who are close to 30, the moving-out date won't come too soon. That's not knocking them. It's just the reality of the times we are living in.

'I really don't want to wait until the date to come up with solutions. I have thought about it and this is where I want to be with my finances at the very least:

- No credit card debt

- At least $1000 unaccounted for in my bank account

- At least $1000 in a savings account

- All baby product purchases accounted for (crib, stroller, car seat etc.)

- A savings plan for the baby started

'Sounds simple, right? Not so fast. Some expenses are accounted for like gas, mortgage, heat, and so on. But unexpected expenses come up all the time: taxes, car repairs, house repairs, medical expenses, weddings, funerals, etc. The world is full of lovely little expenditures that you don't foresee. I have also never claimed to be a financial wizard and I don't see my job giving me a massive raise for me being me.

'So, I am going to go see a financial advisor and try to get as many ducks in a row as I can. Hopefully he'll be able to set me and my family on the right path without me having to get a second job.'

After the baby actually arrives after a traumatic birth, his whole attitude changes and he goes from thinking and planning about having enough money to worrying about the baby's welfare.

'As soon as that little baby came out crying, breathing, beautiful, with 10 fingers and 10 toes, I was finally able to breathe a sigh of relief myself. I was in awe, and still am. She was the most perfect thing I had ever seen and I helped make her. At that moment I knew she was mine and nothing bad was ever going to happen to her ever again.'

I often wonder if the children of people who write these sorts of Internet posts read back what their parents wrote while they were in the womb.

I bet this baby will be surprised about how concerned her dad was with 'affording' to have her, when, on the day, the traumatic birth and rush to the hospital with the chance that she and her mother might not survive paled in comparison.

Here Pisces white witch Nadine tells us what it was like having a Taurus dad. As we found out earlier, her husband is also Taurus.

Growing Up with a Taurean Dad:

'Having a Taurus for a Dad is great when you are looking for Solomon-like advice – my Dad could always get the balance right between encouraging me to go for it and playing devil's advocate to ensure I was committed!

'On the home front, our home was definitely my Dad's castle – no friends or boyfriends were allowed upstairs – that was private territory! On the plus side he was always welcoming to friends and visitors, would always tell a joke or two and be charming, and would never embarrass a sensitive Piscean teenager!'

Both of Nadine's parents are Earth signs (her mother is a Capricorn), so Nadine was surrounded by practical, earthy energies, which kept her Pisces fluffiness in check.

Your Taurus Sibling

As I have said before, if you want to get along well with someone, it helps if you're the same or complementary elements. If you have a Taurus sibling and you are an Earth or Water sign, getting along will be much easier.

As before, being a Fire or Air sign might result in misunderstandings. One thing is for sure, don't borrow their toys or invade their space.

A Taurus likes to surround themselves at home with reassurance in the way of clothing, belongings, food, tools and equipment that is needed for their hobbies, and if you gaily move any, or use them yourself, without permission, you will create a lot of conflict.

If you have to share rooms, make sure you clearly delineate what is what and who goes where. Keep in mind that you're dealing with an Earth sign. With someone who lives on this wonderful planet of ours and enjoys connecting with all that it can offer in a practical way. They're not interested too much in your ideas or thoughts. They are much more concerned with your actions.

Remember the old saying: 'Actions speak louder than words'? It must have been written by a Taurus!

Marianne tells us about the things she enjoys about her older Taurus brother:

> 'So, I'm going to get sappy for a moment. Today, May 19th, is my older brother's birthday. I believe my brother embodies all the positive qualities of a Taurus: smooth, caring, protective, funny, comforting etc.
>
> 'He can also be stubborn as hell. But he's the reason why I love Taurus people so much. He helped raise me when my father wasn't always around, and my brother has now turned out to be a wonderful father himself. Sometimes I joke that if I could find any guy who is half the man my brother is I'd be pretty content. So, I wish my bull-headed brother a happy 29th birthday and more to come.'

Obviously, Capricorn Marianne has a good relationship with her brother. Not everyone will get on as well as they do, but provided you take into account the tips I've already passed on, you'll do well. If you are Fire or Air make sure you don't spend too much time together and get on each other's nerves.

I hope you have enjoyed reading and learning about the 2nd sign of the Zodiac. I hope you have managed to make a birth chart using the astro.com website. I also hope this book has sparked an interest in one of the oldest divination methods in the world.

I wish you well on your life's journey. If we all understood each other better, the world would be a happier place.

Astrological Chart Information and Birth Data

(from astro-databank at www.astro.com and www.astrotheme.com)

No accurate birth data (times missing)

Florence Nightingale, 12th May 1820, Florence, Italy, Sun Taurus, Moon Taurus

Anthony Trollope, 24th April 1815, London, UK

Enya, Eithne Ní Bhraonáin, 17th May 1961, County Donegal, Ireland, Sun Taurus, Moon Gemini

David Servan-Schreiber, 21st April 1961, Hauts-de-Seine, France, Sun Taurus, Moon Cancer

Adele, 5th May 1988, London, Sun Taurus, Moon Sagittarius (Sun conjunct Jupiter)

Ascendant

Sue Grafton, 24th April 1940, Louisville, Kentucky, USA, 4.10pm, Aries Ascendant, Sun in 1st, Moon Sagittarius

George Lucas, 14th May 1944, Modesto, CA, USA, 5.40am, Taurus Ascendant, Sun in 1st, Moon Aquarius

Michele Pfeiffer, 29th April 1958, Santa Ana, California, USA, 8.11am, Gemini Ascendant, Sun in 11th, Moon Virgo

James M. Barrie, 9th May 1860, Kirriemuir, Scotland, UK, 6.30am, Cancer Ascendant, Sun in 11th, Moon Capricorn

Al Pacino, 25th April 1940, Manhattan, New York, USA, 11.02am, Leo Ascendant, Sun in 10th, Moon Sagittarius

Shirley MacLaine, 24th April 1934, Richmond, VA, USA, 3.57pm, Virgo Ascendant, Sun in 8th, Moon Virgo

Harper Lee, 28th April 1926, Monroeville, AL, USA, 5.25pm, Libra Ascendant, Sun in 7th, Moon Scorpio

Sigmund Freud, 6th May 1856, Pribor, Czech Republic, 6.30pm, Scorpio Ascendant, Sun in 7th, Moon Gemini

Leonardo da Vinci, 14th April 1452 (Julian calendar), Vinci, Italy, 9.40pm, Sagittarius Ascendant, Sun in 5th, Moon Pisces

Malcolm X, 19th May, 1925, Omaha, NE, USA, 10.25pm, Capricorn Ascendant, Sun in 5th, Moon Aries

Queen Elizabeth II, Queen of England, 21st April 1926, London, England, 2.40am, Capricorn Ascendant, Sun in 4th, Moon Leo

Karl Marx, 5th May 1818, Trier, Germany, 2am, Aquarius Ascendant, Sun in 3rd, Moon Taurus

Moon

Stevie Wonder, 13th May 1950, Saginaw, MI, USA, 4.15pm, Libra Ascendant, Sun in 8th, Moon Aries

Katharine Hepburn, 12th May 1907, Hartford, CT, USA, 5.47pm, Scorpio Ascendant, Sun in 7th, Moon Taurus

Barbra Streisand, 24th April 1942, Brooklyn, Kings County, NY, USA, 5.08am, Aries Ascendant, Sun in 1st, Moon Leo

Pete Townshend, 19th May 1945, London, England, UK, 3pm, Virgo Ascendant, Sun in 9th, Moon Virgo

Jordan Knight, 17th May 1970, Worcester, MA, USA, 4.50am, Taurus Ascendant, Sun in 1st, Moon Libra

Bono (Paul David Hewson), 10th May 1960, Dublin, Ireland, 2am, Capricorn Ascendant, Sun in 4th, Moon Scorpio

Andy Murray, 15th May 1987, Glasgow, Scotland, UK, 2.10pm, Virgo Ascendant, Sun in 9th, Moon Sagittarius

David Beckham, 2nd May 1975, London, England, UK, 6.17am, Taurus Ascendant, Sun in 12th, Moon Capricorn

Orson Welles, 6th May 1915, Kenosha, WI, USA, 7am, Gemini Ascendant, Sun in 11th, Moon Aquarius

Houses

Barry Crump, 15th May 1935, Papatoetoe, New Zealand, 3am, Aries Ascendant, Sun in 2nd, Moon Libra

Robert Browning, 7th May 1812, Camberwell, England, UK, 10pm, Sagittarius Ascendant, Sun in 6th, Moon Aries

Joanna Lumley, 1st May 1946, Srinagar, India, 7.30pm, Scorpio Ascendant, Sun in 7th, Moon Taurus

Salvador Dali, 11th May 1904, Figueras, Spain, 8.34am, Cancer Ascendant, Sun in 10th, Moon Aries

William Lilly, 1st May 1602 (Julian calendar) Diseworth, England, UK, 2am, Pisces Ascendant, Sun in 3rd, Moon Capricorn

Immanuel Kant, 22nd April 1724, Konisberg/Ostpreussen, Germany, 5am, Taurus Ascendant, Sun in 12th, Moon Aries

Further Information

The Astrological Association www.astrologicalassociation.com

The Bach Centre, The Dr Edward Bach Centre, Mount Vernon, Bakers Lane, Brightwell-cum-Sotwell, Oxon, OX10 0PZ, UK www.bachcentre.com

Ethical Dating Site www.natural-friends.com

Spiritual Community in North Scotland www.findhorn.org

References

1. Christopher McIntosh, *The Astrologers and Their Creed: An Historical Outline*, Arrow Books, London, 1971

2./7. Nicholas Campion, *The Dawn of Astrology, Volume 1: The Ancient and Classical Worlds*, Continuum Books, London, 2008 www.continuumbooks.com

3. Diane Wolkstein and Samuel Noah Kramer, *Inanna, Queen of Heaven and Earth: Her Stories and Hymns from Sumer*, Harper Perennial, New York, 1983

4. Paul Sutherland, *Essential Astronomy: A Beginner's Guide to the Sky at Night*, Igloo Books, 2007

5. Clare Gibson, *The Handbook of Astronomy: Guide to the Night Sky*, Kerswell Books, 2009

6. http://www.gutenberg.org/ebooks/1045

8./9. Colin Evans, *The New Waites Compendium of Natal Astrology*, edited by Brian E. F. Gardener, Routledge and Kegan Paul, London, 1967

10. Caroline Casey, *Making the Gods Work for You: The Astrological Language of the Psyche*, Three Rivers Press, 1999

11. Bil Tierney, *All Around the Zodiac: Exploring Astrology's Twelve Signs*, Llewellyn Publications, 2001

12. Felix Lyle and Brian Aspland, *The Instant Astrologer*, Judy Piakus Publishers, London, 1998

13. Rae Orion, *Astrology for Dummies*, IDG Books Worldwide, Inc., Foster City, CA, 1999

14. http://en.wikipedia.org/wiki/Sigmund_Freud#Escape_from_Nazism

15. http://nursingplanet.com/Nightingale/taking_food.html

16. http://en.wikiquote.org/wiki/Leonardo_da_Vinci

17. http://www.guide2bristol.com/news/1865/Bristol-RWA-artist-interview-David-Shepherd

Dodona Books offers a broad spectrum of divination systems to suit all, including Astrology, Tarot, Runes, Ogham, Palmistry, Dream Interpretation, Scrying, Dowsing, I Ching, Numerology, Angels and Faeries, Tasseomancy and Introspection.